Easy Diabetic Recipes

Delicious & Healthy Meals in Minutes

Sally N. Hunt, Ph.D.

Cookbook Resources LLC
Highland Village, Texas

Easy Diabetic Recipes
Delicious & Healthy Meals in Minutes

1st Printing - March 2008
2nd Printing - September 2008
3rd Printing - August 2009
4th Printing - April 2010

International Standard Book No. 978-1-59769-012-6

Library of Congress Control No. 2009931876

Library of Congress Cataloging-in-Publication Data

    Hunt, Sally N.
     Easy diabetic recipes : delicious & healthy meals in minutes / Sally N. Hunt.
      p. cm.
     Includes index.
     ISBN 978-1-59769-012-6
     1. Diabetes--Diet therapy--Recipes. 2. Quick and easy cookery. 3. Cookery, American. I. Title.

               2009931876

Cover by Nancy Bohanan

Edited, Designed, Published and Manufactured in the United States of America by
Cookbook Resources, LLC
541 Doubletree Drive
Highland Village, Texas 75077

Toll free 866-229-2665

www.cookbookresources.com

Bringing Family and Friends to the Table

About the Recipe Collection

E asy *Diabetic Recipes* is not just for individuals with diabetes, but for anyone seeking a healthier way of eating. One of my goals is to help readers develop awareness of nutrient values, especially amounts of unhealthy sugars and carbohydrates in foods.

Ingredients were selected to reduce refined sugars and carbohydrates as well as overall calories, fat, cholesterol and sodium. There are favorite recipes to enjoy without worrying about overloading on "carbs".

Simple and easy to understand procedures and techniques are used. You should have no difficulty with these healthy, delicious recipes. They are quickly prepared, which saves time in the kitchen.

Keep your pantry and refrigerator stocked with frequently used products so you can prepare a healthy dish at a moment's notice.

"Nutrition Facts" are listed with each recipe in the same format as nutrition labels on purchased foods. Be sure to check the serving sizes on the recipes to help with portion control.

Nutrition labeling is one of the most important tools available to you. Not only does it give accurate nutrient information, but also the number of servings and serving size of a food product.

It's exciting to offer readers this collection of healthy, delicious and easy recipes.

Here's to your lifelong health!

Sally N. Hunt, Ph.D.

For more about Dr. Hunt, please see page 20.

Contents

Contents

Food and Drug Administration (FDA) Nutrition Labeling

Nutrition Facts Label

If you learn to use the Nutrition Facts label, you will have an excellent source of knowledge to help you plan your daily food intake. It may take some practice to learn how to use the label effectively, but it will be worth it

The circled numbers by the below example of a Nutrition Facts label refer to the numbers shown with each explanation.

① **Serving Size**

Serving sizes are given in familiar units such as cups or pieces and also in metric measures. *See Nutrition Label at right. Example:* Serving Size 1 cup (266g).

② **Servings Per Container**

The label states how many servings of the food are in the package so you can plan how to use the food in a recipe or how much of the product you need to purchase.

Nutrition Facts	
① Serving Size 1 cup (266 g)	
② Servings Per Container about 2	
③ **Amount Per Serving**	
④ **Calories** 130 Calories from Fat 20 ⑤	
% Daily Value* ⑥	
⑦ **Total Fat** 2g	3%
Saturated Fat 1g	
Trans Fat 0g	
⑧ **Cholesterol** 10mg	9%
⑨ **Sodium** 890mg	37%
⑩ **Total Carbohydrate** 19g	6%
⑪ Dietary Fiber 4g	16%
⑫ Sugars 4g	
⑬ **Protein** 8g	
⑭ Vitamin A 60% • Vitamin C 2%	
Calcium 2% • Iron 6%	
⑮ *Percent Daily Values are based on a 2,000 calorie diet. Your daily values may be higher or lower depending on your calorie needs.	

See Nutrition Label above. Example: Servings Per Container about 2.

③ Amount Per Serving

This headline alerts you to the nutrient values in a single serving of the food. *See Nutrition Label, page 6.*

④ Calories

Calories are a measure of food energy or how much fuel your body can utilize from a single serving of the food. Many of us consume more calories than we need without getting the nutrients our bodies actually need. *See Nutrition Label, page 6. Example:* **Calories** 130.

⑤ Calories from Fat

This tells you how many of the total calories are from fat. *See Nutrition Label, page 6. Example:* Calories from Fat 20.

⑥ Percent (%) Daily Value

The percentages on the right side of the label refer to a standard Percent Daily Value based on a 2,000 calorie diet. Your Daily Value may be higher or lower depending on your individual calorie needs. *See Nutrition Label, page 6. Example: Total Fat 2g is 3% of the recommended % Daily Value for fat.*

⑦ Total Fat

Most recipes in this book are generally low in fat. Some of the recipes actually have zero (0) grams of fat! Fat is measured in grams (g). Total Fat also **includes** the amounts of Saturated Fat and Trans Fat in the food. *See Nutrition Label, page 6. Example:* **Total Fat** 2g.

⑧ Cholesterol

Cholesterol is measured in milligrams (mg). Health experts recommend adults reduce cholesterol intake to less than 300 milligrams daily.

To maintain a healthy cholesterol intake, these recipes use liquid egg substitute and products that are reduced-fat or fat-free.

See Nutrition Label, page 6. Example: **Cholesterol** 10mg.

⑨ Sodium

Although many of us do not have to limit salt intake, health experts still advise limiting daily salt intake to less than 6 grams, the equivalent of 2,400 milligrams of sodium. Only 1 teaspoon (5 grams) of salt contributes 2,000 mg sodium to the body.

Due to the high amounts of sodium in many foods, salt is not used as an ingredient in the recipes in this book. In general, processed foods contain the most sodium compared to fresh unprocessed foods.

Sodium is measured in milligrams (mg). *See Nutrition Label, page 6. Example:* **Sodium** 890mg. *In this example, over one-third of the daily sodium intake is used in this single serving of a processed food.*

⑩ Total Carbohydrate

Dietary recommendations are that carbohydrates should provide more than half of our daily energy (calories) intake. A variety of whole grains, vegetables, fruits and legumes (dried beans and peas) should be chosen daily.

The recipes include whole grain products, whole wheat breads, whole wheat tortillas, whole wheat pasta and brown rice in addition to a wide selection of fresh vegetables and fruits. Choose low-carb and reduced-fat products if they are available.

Carbohydrate is measured in grams (g). *See Nutrition Label, page 6. Example:* **Total Carbohydrate** 19g.

⑪ Dietary Fiber

The FDA recommends healthy adults consume 25 grams of dietary fiber daily. Dietary Fiber is measured in grams (g). Note that the grams of Total Carbohydrate on the label **include** the grams of fiber. *See Nutrition Label, page 6. Example:* Dietary Fiber 4g.

Where to get more fiber? Whole-grain products provide about 1 to 2 grams (or more) of fiber per serving, such as 1 slice whole wheat bread.

Most vegetables contain about 2 to 3 grams of fiber per ½ cup serving of cooked vegetable. Fresh fruits have about 2 grams of fiber per serving, such as 1 medium apple. About 8 grams of fiber are provided in ½ cup of cooked beans.

⑫ Sugars

According to experts, added sugars should contribute only 10 percent of energy intake (calories) per day. Foods that contain added sugar (cookies, cakes, sodas, etc.) generally contain lots of calories, but very few needed nutrients.

Fortunately, sugar substitutes are widely available today for use by individuals who desire sweetness in foods, without the added calories of sugar and other sweeteners. The recipes in this book generally use sugar substitutes instead of sugar.

Sugars are measured in grams (g). Note that the grams of Total Carbohydrate on the label **include** the grams of sugar. *See Nutrition Label, page 6. Example:* Sugars 4g.

⑬ **Protein**

These recipes include a variety of protein sources that are low in fat and calories. On the Nutrition Facts label, the amount of protein in a single serving of food is given in grams. *See Nutrition Label, page 6. Example:* **Protein** 8g.

⑭ **Additional Information**

Most labels also include information about some of the vitamins and minerals in the food. *See Nutrition Label, page 6.*

⑮ **Standard 2,000 Calorie Diet**

Nutrition labels include a note of explanation that the Nutrition Facts are based on the FDA standard of a 2,000 calorie diet. Some labels also include information for a 2,500 calorie diet.

See Nutrition Label, page 6. Your personal calorie needs as determined by a health professional may be different from the FDA's standard used for Nutrition Facts labels.

Sources:

American Dietetic Association. www.ada.org

U.S. Food and Drug Administration, Center for Food Safety and Applied Nutrition. www.cfsan.fda.gov

Whitney, E. N. & S. R. Rolfes. *Understanding Nutrition,* 9th ed., 2002. Wadsworth Group, Thomson Learning, Inc.

Ingredients

Beef

Ground beef in the recipes should be lean or extra lean. Meat labels now include the percentage of fat.

In 3½ ounces (100g) of ground beef, the percentages of lean meat and fat and calories are:

Percentages of Lean Meat and Fat (3.5 oz; 100g)	Calories
95% lean meat, 5% fat	137
90% lean meat, 10% fat	176
85% lean meat, 15% fat	215
80% lean meat, 20% fat	254

Butter and Margarine

Most of the recipes specify reduced-fat margarine. However, there are several recipes that include butter. Since margarines containing trans fats have been found to be harmful to the body, you may wish to cook with butter.

The relatively new fat replacers have some or all functions of fat and may or may not provide calories.

Olestra is a synthetic fat with 0 calories per gram. Regular fats have 9 calories per gram. The FDA has approved olestra as an additive in snack foods such as potato chips, crackers and tortilla chips.

Cheese

Cheese – Cheddar

Reduced-fat cheddar cheese is generally specified in the recipes.

Cheeses such as reduced-fat Colby Jack and part-skim Mozzarella may work interchangeably with cheddar, but have a different flavor. Some fat-free cheeses and soy-protein cheeses have different melting ability compared to reduced-fat cheese.

Cheese – Cream Cheese

Reduced-fat cream cheese is sold in 8-ounce packages and is usually soft enough straight from the refrigerator to combine with other ingredients. Whipped reduced-fat cream cheese generally works well in recipes that specify use of reduced-fat cream cheese.

Cheese – Feta, Blue, Gorgonzola

These cheeses provide zesty, hearty flavors in small amounts.

Cheese – Parmesan and Romano

Dry parmesan cheese in shaker containers is an economical convenience. However, parmesan grated right before use is especially delicious. In the recipes, they are generally interchangeable.

Chicken Breast Halves

Throughout the recipes, "chicken breast halves" are used. Select boneless, skinless chicken breast halves.

Four ounces (112g) of boneless, skinless chicken breast half yields 110 calories and 2.5 grams fat. The

same amount with skin and ribs yields 130 calories
and 4 grams fat.

Chicken Broth

Chicken broth is used throughout the recipes. Purchase
canned 98% fat-free chicken broth or prepare homemade
broth. Canned and homemade chicken broths are
preferable to bouillon-based crystals or cubes with high
sodium levels.

Egg Substitutes

The recipes use egg substitutes. Refrigerated liquid egg
substitute and liquid egg whites work well in recipes.

One-fourth cup liquid egg substitute is equal to one
egg. Consult the manufacturer for various uses in cooking
and baking.

Green Chilies

Convenience and shelf life are advantages of using
canned green chilies. You may purchase both chopped
and whole green chilies in 4-ounce cans.

Fresh New Mexico green chilies (or Anaheim green
chilies) are excellent choices for cooking. Prior to use in
cooking, roast the fresh chilies to remove the skins.

Green Onions (Scallions)

Green onions add fresh, zesty flavor to the recipes. Use
both the white part and the green tops when called for in
a recipe. Look for green onions that are thin and uniform
in size. Strip off any wilted parts and use a sharp wide-
blade knife for easier chopping.

Herbs

Fresh herbs are an excellent way to add flavor to a dish. Choose fresh herbs for best flavor or crush dried herbs to release flavor. Herb blends are convenient and are frequently used in the recipes.

Non-stick Cooking Spray

To avoid fat content of oils, butter and shortening, cooking sprays are used in the recipes. Canola oil and olive oil sprays are good choices.

Oils

Canola oil is used almost exclusively in the recipes. Other oils considered good choices are safflower oil, sunflower oil, corn oil and olive oil

Salt

Salt and salt substitutes generally are not listed as ingredients. It is your choice whether or not to add salt or salt substitute. Health experts recommend sodium intakes of less than 2,400 milligrams per day, which is about one teaspoon of salt.

Seasoning Blends

Many recipes list seasoning blends as ingredients. Creole and Cajun seasoning blends are frequently used. Some of these products are salt-free or low in salt, but generally provide a substantial amount of sodium and should be used moderately.

Sugar Substitutes

In the recipes, "Sugar substitute equal to 2 teaspoons (10 ml) sugar," refers to the amount of sugar substitute that is equal to the SWEETNESS in 2 teaspoons sugar, not necessarily the volume of 2 teaspoons.

The FDA has approved safety of these low calorie sweeteners:

Sugar Substitute	Some Brand Names	Details
Saccharin	Sweet'N Low® Sugar Twin®	Saccharin can be used to sweeten both hot and cold foods.
Aspartame	NutraSweet® Equal®	High temperatures can decrease sweetness of aspartame. Contact the manufacturer for recommended use of aspartame in baking and cooking.
Acesulfame K (potassium)	Sweet One® Swiss Sweet® Sunette®	This sweetener is heat stable and can be used in baking and cooking.
Sucralose	Splenda®	Sucralose is not affected by heat and retains sweetness in hot beverages, baked goods and processed foods.

Tortillas

In the recipes, 8-inch low-carbohydrate whole wheat tortillas are generally used.

What is a "healthy" food?

In the cookbook, a "healthy" food is one that is low in fat, cholesterol, refined sugars, sodium and overall calories, yet provides a balance of nutrients. Fresh, natural, unprocessed and frozen foods are generally considered better choices than are canned, pre-packaged and processed foods.

What kind of products should I buy to help me reduce calories, refined sugars, fat, cholesterol and sodium? Look for the following labels on pre-packaged foods.

To reduce calories, choose:

* Calorie free
* Low calorie
* Reduced calorie

To reduce fat, saturated fat and cholesterol, choose:

* Fat free
* Low fat
* Less fat
* Low saturated
* Less saturated
* Cholesterol free
* Low cholesterol
* Less cholesterol
* Extra lean
* Lean
* Light
* Lite

To reduce sugars, choose:

* Sugar free
* Lite sugar free
* Low sugar
* No sugar added
* Sugar substitute
* Sugar replacer
* Artificial sweetener

To reduce sodium, choose:

* No salt
* Salt free
* Light or lite
* Sodium free
* Low sodium
* Light in sodium
* Very low sodium
* Very low sodium

Begin to Think in Metric

You'll notice that metric measurements are given in each recipe. This not only helps our readers who use the metric system, but helps those using the U.S. standard measurement system become aware of cooking with metrics. The following table gives equivalents of metric weight in grams and volume.

Important: Avoirdupois ounces (weight) are NOT the same as fluid ounces (volume) in the U.S. system.

Weight: Grams (g)

1 g = 1000 milligrams (mg)
1 g = 0.035 ounces (oz)
1 oz = 28.35 g or = 30 g
100 g = 3.53 oz
1 kilogram (kg) = 1000 g
1 kg = 2.2 pounds (lbs)
453.6 g = 1 lb

Volume: Liters (L)

1 L = 1000 milliliters (ml)
0.95 L = 1 quart (32 fluid ounces)
1 ml = 0.034 fluid ounces
236.6 ml = 1 cup (8 fluid ounces)

Metric Factoids

A half-cup of vegetables weighs about 100 to
120 grams.

A liter (liquid) is approximately one U.S. quart.

Eight fluid ounces (1 cup) are generally rounded to
250 milliliters.

Four fluid ounces (½ cup) are generally rounded to
125 milliliters.

A 5-pound bag of potatoes weighs about
2.27 kilograms.

A 176-pound person weighs about 80 kilograms.

About the Author

Sally N. Hunt earned her Ph.D. at Texas Woman's University, M.S. at Northwestern State University of Louisiana and B.S. at the University of Oklahoma. The areas of study and research were in Home Economics Education, with concentration in foods and nutrition.

Sally N. Hunt, Ph.D.

For 25 years, she was a Teacher Educator and Administrator at the university level. Hunt taught home economics education, foods and nutrition classes from high school through college levels. She has appeared on local television programs and the QVC network. She continues to reach the public through health programs and classes.

Her published cookbooks are *Easy Healthy Cooking with 4 Ingredients*, *Easy Diabetic Cooking with 4 Ingredients* and *365 Easy Vegetarian Recipes*.

Appetizers
&
Beverages

Appetizers & Beverages Contents

Turkey Tortilla Bites

½ pound ground white turkey	230 g
¾ cup mild red enchilada sauce	160 g
6 (8 inch) low-carb whole wheat tortillas	6 (20 cm)
1 cup finely shredded reduced-fat cheddar cheese	115 g

1. Preheat oven to 375° (190° C).

2. Cook and stir turkey for about 8 to 10 minutes in nonstick skillet over medium heat. Add enchilada sauce and simmer for about 5 minutes over medium-low heat.

3. Spray both sides of each tortilla and spread 2 tablespoons turkey mixture on each tortilla, spreading close to edge. Top each with 4 teaspoons cheese. Roll tightly and secure with toothpick.

4. Arrange filled tortillas on sprayed baking sheet and bake for about 3 minutes or just until cheese melts. Cut each tortilla into quarters, securing with toothpicks.

Nutrition Facts		
Size of serving 2 tortilla bites Servings Per Recipe 12		
Amount of Serving		
Calories 26		
Total Fat 1g		
Cholesterol 7mg		
Sodium 40mg		
Total Carbohydrate 1g		
Dietary Fiber 1g		
Sugars 0g		
Protein 3g		

Hot Asparagus Rolls

10 - 20 fresh asparagus spears, trimmed
10 slices sugar-free wheat bread, crusts
    trimmed
10 teaspoons reduced-fat mayonnaise   50 ml
5 part-skim mozzarella string cheese sticks,
    pulled apart

1. Cook asparagus in 1 inch (2.5 cm) boiling water in
    10-inch (25 cm) skillet. Drain well and set aside.

2. With rolling pin, slightly flatten bread slices. Spread
    about 1 teaspoon (5 ml) mayonnaise
    on one side of each bread slice.

3. Top with 1 or 2 asparagus spears and
    3 to 4 cheese strings. Roll carefully.

4. Arrange rolls seam-side down on
    sprayed baking sheet.

5. Broil for 3 to 5 minutes about
    5 inches (13 cm) from heat until
    bread toasts.

Nutrition Facts
Serving Size 1 roll
Servings per Recipe 10
Amount Per Serving
Calories 110
Total Fat 3g
Cholesterol 6mg
Sodium 218mg
Total Carbohydrate 4g
Dietary Fiber 3g
Sugars 1g
Protein 7g

Hearty Cocktail Meatballs

1 (1 pound) lean ground beef	455 g
1 (10 ounce) can 98% fat-free cream of	
mushroom soup	280 g
1 cup long grain rice	185 g
⅓ cup finely chopped onion	55 g
2 tablespoons chopped fresh parsley	8 g

1. Preheat oven to 350° (175° C).

2. Combine all ingredients and mix well.

3. Form mixture into balls of about 2 tablespoons (18 g) each. (For easier handling, spray hands with non-stick cooking spray and scoop and pack mixture into ice cream scoop.)

4. Arrange meatballs in sprayed 8-inch (20 cm) square baking dish. Cover and bake for 1 hour or until rice is tender.

5. Uncover and bake for 10 minutes or until meatballs brown. Drain on paper towels.

TIP: Serve with Easy Pasta Sauce (page 235).

Nutrition Facts
Serving Size 1 meatball (not including sauce) Servings per Recipe 12
Amount Per Serving
Calories 140
Total Fat 4g
Cholesterol 34mg
Sodium 126mg
Total Carbohydrate 16g
Dietary Fiber less than 1g
Sugars less than 1g
Protein 9g

Saucy Chicken Wings

20 chicken wings
1 cup Low-Carb Barbecue Sauce (page 235)   250 ml
1 cup Ranch-Style Buttermilk Dressing
    (page 139)   250 ml

1. Preheat oven to 325° (160° C).

2. Rinse and dry chicken wings with paper towels.

3. Arrange chicken wings on sprayed foil-lined baking sheet.

4. Brush wings with barbecue sauce and bake for about 30 minutes.

5. Turn wings over and brush other side with sauce. Return to oven and bake for an additional 30 minutes or until chicken is fork tender and crisp. Serve with dressing.

Nutrition Facts
Serving Size 2 wings with 1 tablespoon (15 ml) dressing
Servings Per Recipe 10
Amount Per Serving
Calories 276
Total Fat 20g
Cholesterol 79mg
Sodium 277mg
Total Carbohydrate 6g
Dietary Fiber 0g
Sugars 4g
Protein 18g

Get Your Veggies Nachos

4 cups cut vegetables (choose from celery and carrot sticks, squash slices, bell pepper strips, cauliflower and/or broccoli florets)	420 g
1½ cups finely shredded reduced-fat cheddar or Jack cheese	170 g
2 - 3 tablespoons canned mild diced green chilies, drained	30 - 45 g
2 - 3 tablespoons sliced ripe olives, drained	15 - 25 g

1. Preheat broiler.

2. Arrange vegetable pieces on ovenproof serving platter and sprinkle with cheese, green chilies and olives.

3. Broil 4 to 6 inches (10 to 15 cm) from heat for about 5 to 7 minutes or until cheese melts.

Nutrition Facts
Serving Size ½ cup (125 ml)
Servings Per Recipe 8
Amount Per Serving
Calories 180
Total Fat 13g
Cholesterol 35mg
Sodium 419mg
Total Carbohydrate 16g
Dietary Fiber 2g
Sugars 3g
Protein 13g

Creamy Shrimp Dip

This delicious dip disappears quickly!

1 (8 ounce) package reduced-fat cream cheese, softened	230 g
½ cup reduced-fat mayonnaise	115 g
1 (6 ounce) can chopped peeled, veined shrimp, drained, rinsed	170 g
1 teaspoon blackened seasoning	5 ml
1 teaspoon fresh lemon juice	5 ml

1. Combine all ingredients in bowl and mix well.

2. Refrigerate for 1 hour before serving.

Nutrition Facts

Serving Size 2
Servings Per Recipe 18

Amount Per Serving

Calories 66

Total Fat 5g

Cholesterol 28mg

Sodium 106mg

Total Carbohydrate 16g

Dietary Fiber 0g

Sugars less than 1g

Protein 3g

Low-Carb Chili Cheese Squares

4 cups finely shredded reduced-fat cheddar cheese	455 g
1 cup liquid egg substitute	245 g
1 (4 ounce) can mild diced green chilies, drained	115 g
⅓ cup finely chopped green onions with tops	30 g

1. Preheat oven to 325° (160° C).

2. Mix all ingredients and spread in sprayed 8-inch (20 cm) square baking dish.

3. Bake for 30 minutes or until knife inserted in middle comes out clean.

4. Cut into 1½-inch (3 cm) squares.

Nutrition Facts
Serving Size 1 square
Servings Per Recipe 25
Amount Per Serving
Calories 128
Total Fat 9g
Cholesterol 26mg
Sodium 419mg
Total Carbohydrate 2g
Dietary Fiber 1g
Sugars less than 1g
Protein 10g

Low-Fat Hummus

1 (16 ounce) can garbanzo beans (chickpeas)   455 g
½ cup nonfat plain yogurt   115 g
3 teaspoons fresh lemon juice   15 ml
⅛ - ¼ teaspoon garlic powder   .5 - 1 ml

1. Drain and rinse garbanzo beans in cold water.

2. Add all ingredients to food processor. Process until smooth.

Nutrition Facts
Serving Size 2 tablespoons (30 ml)
Servings Per Recipe 12
Amount Per Serving
Calories 52
Total Fat less than 1g
Cholesterol less than 1mg
Sodium 121mg
Total Carbohydrate 9g
Dietary Fiber 2g
Sugars 3g
Protein 2g

Party Hummus

Low-Fat Hummus (page 30)
¼ cup chopped roasted red pepper or
    diced pimento, drained   65 g/50 g
¼ cup chopped red onion   40 g
¼ cup crumbled feta cheese   40 g

1. Spread hummus evenly in shallow dish or plate and sprinkle with roasted red pepper, red onion and feta cheese.

TIP: *Serve with pita bread wedges or crisp breadsticks.*

Nutrition Facts
Serving Size ¼ cup (60 ml)
Servings Per Recipe 10
Amount Per Serving
Calories 81
Total Fat 2g
Cholesterol 3mg
Sodium 204mg
Total Carbohydrate 13g
Dietary Fiber 2g
Sugars 4g
Protein 4g

Favorite Artichoke Dip

2 (8.5 ounce) cans artichoke hearts in water, drained, chopped	2 (240 g)
1 (4 ounce) can mild diced green chilies, drained	115 g
6 tablespoons reduced-fat mayonnaise	85 g
1½ cups finely shredded reduced-fat cheddar cheese	170 g

1. Preheat oven to 350° (175° C).

2. Spread chopped artichokes in sprayed 9-inch (23 cm) square baking dish and top with green chilies.

3. Carefully spread mayonnaise over green chilies and sprinkle with cheese.

4. Cover and bake for 15 minutes or until mixture bubbles.

Nutrition Facts
Serving Size 2 tablespoons (30 ml) Servings Per Recipe 20
Amount Per Serving
Calories 79
Total Fat 6g
Cholesterol 14mg
Sodium 232mg
Total Carbohydrate 3g
Dietary Fiber less than 1g
Sugars less than 1g
Protein 5g

Zesty Spinach Dip

1 (10 ounce) package frozen chopped spinach, thawed, drained	280 g
⅓ cup finely chopped green onions with tops	30 g
1 tablespoon fresh lemon juice	15 ml
1 (8 ounce) carton reduced-fat sour cream	230 g
Dash cayenne pepper	

1. Squeeze spinach between paper towels to completely remove excess moisture.

2. Process all ingredients in food processor or blender until smooth.

3. Cover and refrigerate for at least 2 hours before serving.

Nutrition Facts
Serving Size 2 tablespoons (30 ml)
Servings Per Recipe 16
Amount Per Serving
Calories 23
Total Fat 1g
Cholesterol 5mg
Sodium 34mg
Total Carbohydrate 2g
Dietary Fiber less than 1g
Sugars 1g
Protein 1g

Herbed Pita Crisps

4 whole wheat pita breads
1 tablespoon Italian herb seasoning blend   15 ml

1. Preheat oven to 350° (175° C).

2. Cut each pita bread with sharp knife to make 12 single wedges.

3. Spray wedges on one side and lightly sprinkle with herb blend. Arrange sprayed side up on baking sheet.

4. Bake for 8 to 10 minutes or until wedges lightly brown. Serve immediately or store in airtight container.

Nutrition Facts	
Serving Size 3 wedges	
Servings Per Recipe 16	
Amount Per Serving	
Calories 43	
Total Fat 1g	
Cholesterol 0mg	
Sodium 85mg	
Total Carbohydrate 9g	
Dietary Fiber 1g	
Sugars less than 1g	
Protein 2g	

Easiest Guacamole Dip

2 ripe avocados
1 teaspoon grated onion   5 ml
2 teaspoons fresh lime juice   10 ml
¼ teaspoon garlic powder   1 ml

1. Halve avocados and remove seeds. Cut halves into quarters and peel. Mash avocado with fork in bowl.

2. Add remaining ingredients and mix well.

3. Cover tightly and refrigerate. Serve same day.

Nutrition Facts	
Serving Size ¼ cup (60 ml)	
Servings Per Recipe 4	
Amount Per Serving	
Calories 143	
Total Fat 13g	
Cholesterol 0mg	
Sodium 67mg	
Total Carbohydrate 8g	
Dietary Fiber 6g	
Sugars less than 1g	
Protein 2g	

Disappearing Deviled Eggs

These deviled eggs will disappear quickly!

6 eggs, hard-boiled, peeled
3 tablespoons reduced-fat mayonnaise   40 g
2 teaspoons dijon-style mustard   10 ml
¼ teaspoon Creole or other spicy
    seasoning blend   1 ml
Paprika for garnish

1. Slice eggs in half lengthwise. Carefully remove egg yolk with fork and thoroughly mash in bowl. Add mayonnaise, mustard and seasoning. Beat with fork until mixture is creamy and smooth.

2. Mound egg yolk mixture evenly onto egg white halves. Sprinkle with paprika.

Nutrition Facts
Serving Size 1 half egg Servings Per Recipe 12
Amount Per Serving
Calories 52
Total Fat 4g
Cholesterol 107mg
Sodium 74mg
Total Carbohydrate less than 1g
Dietary Fiber 0g
Sugars less than 1g
Protein 3g

Two Cheese-Sesame Balls

1 (8 ounce) package reduced-fat cream cheese	230 g
2 (8 ounce) packages finely shredded reduced-fat cheddar cheese	2 (230 g)
2 tablespoons finely chopped parsley	10 g
3 tablespoons toasted sesame seeds	25 g

1. Beat cream cheese, cheddar cheese and parsley in bowl. Cover and refrigerate for at least 4 hours.

2. Form cheese mixture into 1-inch (2.5 cm) balls and roll in toasted sesame seeds. Refrigerate.

Nutrition Facts
Serving Size 2 balls
Servings Per Recipe 12
Amount Per Serving
Calories 178
Total Fat 14g
Cholesterol 40mg
Sodium 350mg
Total Carbohydrate 1g
Dietary Fiber less than 1g
Sugars less than 1g
Protein 12g

Reduced-Fat Chicken Spread

1 cup chopped cooked chicken breast	140 g
¼ cup reduced-fat mayonnaise	55 g
½ cup sliced celery	50 g
¼ cup coarsely chopped red bell pepper	40 g
Dash cayenne pepper	

1. Combine all ingredients in food processor or blender just until they mix well.

Nutrition Facts
Serving Size ⅓ cup (75 ml)
Servings Per Recipe 6
Amount Per Serving
Calories 60
Total Fat 2g
Cholesterol 20mg
Sodium 32mg
Total Carbohydrate 2g
Dietary Fiber 0g
Sugars 1g
Protein 7g

Party Cream Cheese Appetizer

½ cup low-sugar apricot fruit spread	160 g
1 tablespoon prepared horseradish	15 ml
1 (8 ounce) package reduced-fat cream cheese	230 g

1. Mix fruit spread, horseradish and ¼ teaspoon (1 ml) pepper in bowl.

2. Spoon over block of cream cheese.

Nutrition Facts
Serving Size 2 tablespoons (30 ml)
Servings Per Recipe 16
Amount Per Serving
Calories 49
Total Fat 3g
Cholesterol 10mg
Sodium 63mg
Total Carbohydrate 4g
Dietary Fiber less than 1g
Sugars 3g
Protein 2g

Avocado-Tuna Spread

2 large avocados, pitted, peeled, slightly mashed
1 (7 ounce) package albacore white tuna in
    water, drained   200 g
2 tablespoons fresh lemon juice   30 ml
2 teaspoons prepared horseradish   10 ml
Dash cayenne pepper

1. Combine all ingredients in bowl and mix well.

2. Cover tightly and refrigerate until serving time.

Nutrition Facts	
Serving Size ¼ cup (60 ml) Servings Per Recipe 8	
Amount Per Serving	
Calories 90	
Total Fat 6g	
Cholesterol 11mg	
Sodium 98mg	
Total Carbohydrate 4g	
Dietary Fiber 2g	
Sugars 0g	
Protein 7g	

Quick Pesto Toasts

Enjoy the rich taste of pesto without the fat!

10 pieces (2 x 4 inch) melba toast   10 (5 x 10 cm)
3 tablespoons Reduced-Fat Pesto
    Spread (page 232)   45 ml

1. Spread each melba toast piece with 1 teaspoon pesto spread.

Nutrition Facts	
Serving Size 1 melba toast piece Servings Per Recipe 10	
Amount Per Serving	
Calories 24	
Total Fat 0g	
Cholesterol 0mg	
Sodium 37mg	
Total Carbohydrate 4g	
Dietary Fiber 0g	
Sugars 0g	
Protein 1g	

Party Bruschetta

Bruschetta derives from an Italian word meaning "to roast over coals". It is a simple, delicious appetizer or can be used as a bread accompaniment to Italian dishes.

4 (½ inch) thick diagonal slices French bread   4 (1.2 cm)
1 garlic clove, cut
8 teaspoons extra-virgin olive oil   40 ml
¼ cup chopped roma tomatoes, drained   45 g

1. Preheat broiler.

2. Toast bread slices on both sides until they brown lightly. Rub each slice gently with garlic clove and drizzle each with about 2 teaspoons (10 ml) oil.

3. To serve, spoon 1 tablespoon (15 ml) tomatoes on each slice.

TIP: Any firm, ripe tomatoes can be used.

Nutrition Facts
Serving Size 1 slice
Servings Per Recipe 4
Amount Per Serving
Calories 131
Total Fat 8g
Cholesterol 0mg
Sodium 153mg
Total Carbohydrate 4g
Dietary Fiber less than 1g
Sugars less than 1g
Protein 2g

Creamy Tortilla Bites

A great party appetizer!

1 (8 ounce) carton reduced-fat whipped cream cheese spread	230 g
2 tablespoons thick non-chunky salsa	35 g
2½ teaspoons chili powder, divided	12 ml
3 tablespoons finely chopped green onions with tops, divided	20 g
8 (8 inch) low carb whole wheat tortillas	8 (20 cm)

1. Beat cream cheese, salsa, 2 teaspoons (10 ml) chili powder and 2 tablespoons (12 g) green onions. Spread ¼ cup (60 ml) on each warmed tortilla, covering to edges.

2. Roll filled tortillas tightly and slice each tortilla into 4 bites. Secure bites with toothpicks.

3. Cover and refrigerate for at least 30 minutes for flavors to blend. Arrange on serving plate and garnish with ½ teaspoon (2 ml) chili powder and 1 tablespoon (15 ml) chopped green onions.

TIP: *Serve with extra salsa. For easy rolling, use regular 8-inch (20 cm) flour tortillas.*

Nutrition Facts
Serving Size 2 bites
Servings Per Recipe 16
Amount Per Serving
Calories 68
Total Fat 4g
Cholesterol 8mg
Sodium 200mg
Total Carbohydrate 9g
Dietary Fiber 5g
Sugars 1g
Protein 3g

Crunchy Chicken Strips with Barbecue Sauce

4 fresh chicken tenders	
1 cup fat-free Italian dressing	250 ml
1 cup whole wheat melba toast crumbs	120 g
6 tablespoons Low-Carb Barbecue Sauce	
(page 235)	90 ml

1. Cut chicken tenders diagonally into 3 pieces. Place chicken pieces in large resealable plastic bag. Cover with dressing and refrigerate for 2 to 3 hours. Remove tenders from bag and drain on wire rack. Discard dressing.

2. When ready to bake, preheat oven to 375° (190° C).

3. Place toast crumbs on pie pan and coat tenders with crumbs. Let stand for 1 minute for crumbs to adhere. Transfer to sprayed baking sheet. Bake for 15 minutes or until crumbs brown and chicken is no longer pink.

4. To serve, arrange 2 chicken pieces and 1 tablespoon (15 ml) Low-Carb Barbecue Sauce on each of 6 small plates.

TIP: *Chicken tenders are easier to cut if slightly frozen.*

Nutrition Facts
Serving Size 2 pieces with 1 tablespoon (15 ml) sauce
Servings Per Recipe 6
Amount Per Serving
Calories 82
Total Fat 0g
Cholesterol 12mg
Sodium 451mg
Total Carbohydrate 13g
Dietary Fiber 0g
Sugars 7g
Protein 6g

Cheese Lovers Stuffed Celery

4 large celery stalks, trimmed
¼ cup blue cheese   35 g
1 (8 ounce) package reduced-fat
    cream cheese   230 g
1 - 2 teaspoons fat-free milk   5 - 10 ml

1. Cut celery into 3-inch pieces.

2. Combine blue cheese, cream
    cheese and 1 to 2 teaspoons
    (5 to 10 ml) milk. Lightly
    pack onto celery pieces.

Nutrition Facts
Serving Size 2 pieces stuffed celery Servings Per Recipe 6
Amount Per Serving
Calories 78
Total Fat 6g
Cholesterol 18mg
Sodium 153mg
Total Carbohydrate 3g
Dietary Fiber 0g
Sugars 1g
Protein 4g

Dippy Dill Dip

2 cups reduced-fat sour cream   480 g
¼ cup chopped onion   40 g
1 tablespoon dried dill weed   15 ml

1. Combine all ingredients in bowl.

Nutrition Facts
Serving Size ¼ cup (60 ml) Servings Per Recipe 8
Amount Per Serving
Calories 109
Total Fat 9g
Cholesterol 61mg
Sodium 123mg
Total Carbohydrate 14g
Dietary Fiber 7g
Sugars 0g
Protein 4g

Hearty Spinach-Artichoke Dip

1 (13 ounce) can artichoke hearts in water, drained, chopped	370 g
1 (10 ounce) package frozen chopped spinach, thawed, drained	280 g
2 cups reduced-fat mayonnaise	450 g
½ cup crumbled feta or blue cheese	70 g
2 garlic cloves, minced	

1. Preheat oven to 325° (160°).

2. Combine all ingredients in medium bowl. Spread in sprayed 8-inch (20 cm) square baking dish.

3. Bake for 1 hour or until bubbly and hot.

Nutrition Facts
Serving Size ¼ cup (60 ml)
Servings Per Recipe 24
Amount Per Serving
Calories 84
Total Fat 7g
Cholesterol 3mg
Sodium 236mg
Total Carbohydrate 4g
Dietary Fiber 1g
Sugars 0g
Protein 2g

Onion-Pepper Antipasto

2 cups thinly sliced onions   230 g
1 cup green bell pepper strips   90 g
1 cup red bell pepper strips   90 g
6 garlic cloves, minced

1. Combine all ingredients in sprayed 10-inch (25 cm) skillet. Cook over medium-high heat for 5 minutes, stirring frequently.

2. Add ¼ cup (60 ml) water and cook over medium-low heat for about 20 minutes or until vegetables are very tender.

Nutrition Facts	
Serving Size ¼ cup (60 ml) Servings Per Recipe 8	
Amount Per Serving	
Calories 26	
Total Fat 0g	
Cholesterol 0mg	
Sodium 3mg	
Total Carbohydrate 6g	
Dietary Fiber 1g	
Sugars 3g	
Protein 1g	

Party Marinated Veggies

1 (16 ounce) carton fresh mushrooms	455 g
1 (6 ounce) can large pitted ripe olives, drained	170 g
1 (14 ounce) can artichoke hearts in water, drained, quartered	400 g
1 (14 ounce) jar hearts of palm, drained	400 g
1 (15 ounce) can baby corn on cob, drained	425 g
½ cup Classic Italian Dressing (page 137)	125 ml

1. Clean mushrooms and halve large mushrooms.

2. Combine all ingredients in bowl and toss to coat. Refrigerate for at least 6 hours.

Nutrition Facts	
Serving Size ¼ cup (60 ml)	
Servings Per Recipe 32	
Amount Per Serving	
Calories 65	
Total Fat 12g	
Cholesterol 0mg	
Sodium 426mg	
Total Carbohydrate 9g	
Dietary Fiber 4g	
Sugars 2g	
Protein 3g	

Easy Swiss Cheese Spread

½ cup reduced-fat mayonnaise	110 g
2 cups shredded reduced-fat Swiss cheese	215 g
2 tablespoons fresh parsley, finely chopped	10 g

1. Mix mayonnaise and cheese in bowl, using just enough for mayonnaise to achieve spreading consistency. Refrigerate until serving time.

2. Before serving, mold spread into mound and sprinkle with parsley.

Nutrition Facts	
Serving Size 1 tablespoon (15 ml)	
Servings Per Recipe 18	
Amount Per Serving	
Calories 43	
Total Fat 3g	
Cholesterol 4mg	
Sodium 78mg	
Total Carbohydrate 1g	
Dietary Fiber 0g	
Sugars 0g	
Protein 3g	

Three Pepper Vegetable Dip

1 cup reduced-fat cottage cheese, drained	225 g
1 cup reduced-fat mayonnaise	225 g
1 (1 ounce) package dry ranch-style dressing mix	30 g
¼ cup finely chopped green bell peppers	40 g
¼ cup finely chopped red bell peppers	40 g
¼ cup finely chopped yellow bell peppers	40 g

1. Combine all ingredients in blender or food processor. Blend until smooth. Refrigerate until ready to serve.

Nutrition Facts

Serving Size 2 tablespoons (30 ml)
Servings Per Recipe 16

Amount Per Serving

Calories 60

Total Fat 5g

Cholesterol 1mg

Sodium 163mg

Total Carbohydrate 2g

Dietary Fiber 0g

Sugars 1g

Protein 2g

Minty Cucumber Dip

1 cucumber, peeled, seeded, finely
    chopped or grated
2 cups fat-free plain yogurt   455 g
1 clove garlic, finely minced
1½ teaspoons chopped fresh mint or
   ½ teaspoon dried mint, crushed   7 ml/2 ml

1. Place cucumber in wire mesh strainer and press firmly with fingers to remove excess moisture. Mix with yogurt, garlic and mint. Place in serving bowl and garnish with 2 to 3 sprigs of fresh mint.

2. Refrigerate for at least 1 hour before serving. Dip is best served the same day as made.

Nutrition Facts
Serving Size 2 tablespoons (30 ml)
Servings Per Recipe 15
Amount Per Serving
Calories 20
Total Fat 0g
Cholesterol 1mg
Sodium 25mg
Total Carbohydrate 3g
Dietary Fiber 0g
Sugars 3g
Protein 2g

Easy Pesto Dip

1 (8 ounce) carton reduced-fat sour cream	230 g
2 tablespoons refrigerated basil pesto	30 g

1. Combine sour cream and pesto in bowl until they blend well.

Nutrition Facts

Serving Size 2 tablespoons (30 ml)
Servings Per Recipe 10

Amount Per Serving

Calories 44

Total Fat 4g

Cholesterol 9mg

Sodium 46mg

Total Carbohydrate 1g

Dietary Fiber 0g

Sugars 0g

Protein 0g

Kickin' Shrimp Dip

2 cups cooked, veined, finely chopped shrimp	280 g
2 tablespoons horseradish	30 g
½ cup chili sauce	135 g
¾ cup fat-free mayonnaise	170 g
1 tablespoon fresh lemon juice	15 ml

1. Combine all ingredients in bowl. Refrigerate for at least 1 hour before serving.

Nutrition Facts

Serving Size 2 tablespoons (30 ml)
Servings Per Recipe 20

Amount Per Serving

Calories 40

Total Fat 2g

Cholesterol 32mg

Sodium 148mg

Total Carbohydrate 3g

Dietary Fiber 0g

Sugars 1g

Protein 3g

Love It Shrimp Dip

1 (8 ounce) package reduced-fat cream cheese, softened	230 g
½ cup reduced-fat mayonnaise	115 g
1 (6 ounce) can shrimp, drained, chopped	170 g
½ teaspoon Creole or Cajun seasoning	2 ml
1 tablespoon fresh lemon juice	15 ml
2 teaspoons chopped fresh parsley	10 ml

1. Beat cream cheese and mayonnaise in bowl.

2. Stir in shrimp, seasoning, lemon juice and parsley. Refrigerate for at least 1 hour before serving.

Nutrition Facts

Serving Size 2 tablespoons (30 ml)
Servings Per Recipe 18

Amount Per Serving
Calories 62
Total Fat 5g
Cholesterol 31mg
Sodium 160mg
Total Carbohydrate 1g
Dietary Fiber 0g
Sugars 0g
Protein 3g

Bacon-Wrapped Water Chestnuts

¼ cup reduced-sodium soy sauce	60 ml
¼ teaspoon cayenne pepper	1 ml
1 (8 ounce) can whole water chestnuts, drained, rinsed	230 g
½ pound turkey bacon, sliced, cut in thirds	230 g

1. Combine soy sauce and cayenne pepper in shallow bowl. Add water chestnuts and marinate for at least 1 hour. Drain; discard marinade.

2. Wrap one-third slice bacon around each water chestnut and fasten with toothpick. Place on rack in shallow pan.

3. Preheat oven broiler and broil for 5 to 7 minutes, turning once.

Nutrition Facts
Serving Size 2 water chestnuts
Servings Per Recipe 15
Amount Per Serving
Calories 64
Total Fat 4g
Cholesterol 15mg
Sodium 485mg
Total Carbohydrate 2g
Dietary Fiber 0g
Sugars 0g
Protein 5g

Spicy Salsa Dip

1 (8 ounce) carton reduced-fat sour cream   230 g
½ cup medium salsa   130 g
½ teaspoon dijon-style mustard   2 ml

1. Combine all ingredients in bowl. Refrigerate for at least 1 hour for flavors to blend.

Nutrition Facts
Serving Size 2 tablespoons (30 ml) Servings Per Recipe 8
Amount Per Serving
Calories 60
Total Fat 4g
Cholesterol 12mg
Sodium 117mg
Total Carbohydrate 2g
Dietary Fiber 0g
Sugars 1g
Protein 1g

Piquant Curry Dip

1 cup reduced-fat sour cream   240 g
⅓ cup reduced-fat mayonnaise   75 g
½ teaspoon curry powder   2 ml
Dash cayenne pepper

1. Combine all ingredients in bowl. Cover and refrigerate for at least 4 hours. Stir again before serving.

Nutrition Facts
Serving Size 2 tablespoons (30 ml) Servings Per Recipe 10
Amount Per Serving
Calories 59
Total Fat 5g
Cholesterol 9mg
Sodium 66mg
Total Carbohydrate 5g
Dietary Fiber 0g
Sugars 0g
Protein 1g

Zesty Onion Dip

1 (8 ounce) package reduced-fat cream cheese, softened	230 g
1 (8 ounce) carton fat-free sour cream	230 g
½ cup reduced-sugar ketchup or chili sauce	135 g
1 (1 ounce) packet dry onion soup mix	30 g
1 tablespoon fresh lemon juice	15 ml

1. Beat cream cheese in bowl until smooth. Stir in remaining ingredients and mix well.

2. Cover and refrigerate for at least 1 hour.

Nutrition Facts
Serving Size 2 tablespoons (30 ml) Servings Per Recipe 20
Amount Per Serving
Calories 52
Total Fat 4g
Cholesterol 11mg
Sodium 273mg
Total Carbohydrate 3g
Dietary Fiber 0g
Sugars 1g
Protein 2g

Parmesan Pita Wedges

4 (6 inch) whole wheat pita breads	4 (15 cm)
⅓ cup finely chopped parsley	20 g
1 teaspoon Italian herb seasoning	5 ml
⅓ cup finely grated fresh parmesan cheese	35 g

1. Preheat oven to 350° (175° C).

2. Cut around outside edge of each whole pita bread with a sharp knife. Carefully open the whole pita into 2 halves. There should be a total of 8 halves.

3. Combine parsley, herb seasoning and parmesan cheese in bowl.

4. Sprinkle each pita half with cheese mixture and cut each half into 4 wedges. There should be a total of 32 wedges.

5. Arrange pita wedges on baking sheet and bake for 12 to 15 minutes or until crisp and golden brown.

Nutrition Facts
Serving Size 4 wedges
Servings Per Recipe 8
Amount Per Serving
Calories 226
Total Fat 5g
Cholesterol 11mg
Sodium 534mg
Total Carbohydrate 36
Dietary Fiber 5g
Sugars 1g
Protein 11g

Pineapple-Cheese Marvel

2 (8 ounce) packages reduced-fat cream cheese, softened	2 (230 g)
1 (8 ounce) can crushed pineapple in juice, drained	230 g
¼ cup finely chopped green pepper	40 g
2 tablespoons chopped fresh parsley	10 g

1. Combine all ingredients in bowl and mix well. Refrigerate.

Nutrition Facts
Serving Size 1 tablespoon (15 ml)
Servings Per Recipe 30
Amount Per Serving
Calories 42
Total Fat 3g
Cholesterol 11mg
Sodium 64mg
Total Carbohydrate 2g
Dietary Fiber 0g
Sugars 1g
Protein 2g

Sugar Snaps for Dipping

1 pound fresh sugar snap peas	455 g
¼ cup reduced-fat sour cream	60 g
¼ cup reduced-fat mayonnaise	55 g
2 tablespoons fresh mint leaves, chopped	10 g

1. Prepare large bowl with ice water to cool peas after cooking. Snap off top and bottom ends of peas and pull strings away from both sides.

2. Place 1 to 2 inches (2.5 to 5 cm) of water in large skillet and bring to boiling over high heat. Add peas and cook for about 30 seconds or until peas are bright green. Drain and immediately place in bowl of ice water to stop cooking; stir gently until cool. Drain ice water.

3. Combine sour cream, mayonnaise and mint in bowl and pour into a small bowl for serving. Arrange peas on bed of ice in rimmed serving platter to serve.

Nutrition Facts
Serving Size 4 peas with dip
Servings Per Recipe 6
Amount Per Serving
Calories 106
Total Fat 5g
Cholesterol 8mg
Sodium 175mg
Total Carbohydrate 12g
Dietary Fiber 3g
Sugars 6g
Protein 4g

Pico de Gallo with a Twist

1 (4 ounce) can chopped green chilies, drained	115 g
1 (4 ounce) can chopped ripe olives, drained	115 g
2 medium tomatoes, diced	
1 medium green pepper, diced	
½ cup finely chopped red onion	80 g
¼ cup coarsely chopped cilantro	5 g
½ cup Best French Dressing (page 132)	125 ml

1. Combine all ingredients in large bowl.

Nutrition Facts

Serving Size 2 tablespoons (30 ml)
Servings Per Recipe 32

Amount Per Serving

Calories 82

Total Fat 7g

Cholesterol 0mg

Sodium 233mg

Total Carbohydrate 5g

Dietary Fiber 1g

Sugars 3g

Protein less than 1g

Apricot-Almond-Cheese Spread

Delicious sweet appetizer.

5 tablespoons reduced-sugar apricot fruit spread	100 g
1 (8 ounce) package reduced-fat cream cheese	230 g
1 tablespoon sliced almonds, toasted	15 ml

1. Heat apricot spread in small saucepan over low heat.

2. Pour over cream cheese block and sprinkle with almonds.

Nutrition Facts

Serving Size 1 tablespoon (15 ml)
Servings Per Recipe 16

Amount Per Serving

Calories 47

Total Fat 3g

Cholesterol 8mg

Sodium 42mg

Total Carbohydrate 4g

Dietary Fiber 0g

Sugars 3g

Protein 2g

Lime-Spiced Tortilla Chips

4 (8 inch) low-carb whole wheat tortillas	4 (20 cm)
½ teaspoon grated lime peel	2 ml
2 tablespoons fresh lime juice	30 ml
2 teaspoons canola oil	10 ml
Sugar substitute to equal 2 teaspoons (10 ml) sugar	

1. Preheat oven to 350° (175° C).

2. Cut each tortilla into 4 wedges for a total of 16 wedges. Spray both sides of each wedge.

3. Combine lime peel, lime juice, oil and sugar substitute. Spread or sprinkle on wedges.

4. Place tortilla wedges on sprayed baking sheet. Bake for 10 to 15 minutes or until crisp.

Nutrition Facts
Serving Size 2 wedges
Servings Per Recipe 8
Amount Per Serving
Calories 34
Total Fat 1g
Cholesterol 0mg
Sodium 80mg
Total Carbohydrate 4g
Dietary Fiber 3g
Sugars 0g
Protein 1g

Raspberry-Pineapple Party Cubes

1 (.3 ounce) package sugar-free raspberry soft drink mix	10 g
Sugar substitute to equal ½ cup (100 g) sugar	
4 cups unsweetened pineapple juice	1 L
3 (12 ounce) cans diet lemon-lime soda, chilled	3 (355 ml)

1. Mix soft drink powder, sugar substitute and juice in large bowl. Pour into 2 ice cube trays and freeze.

2. To serve, place cubes in glasses and fill with diet soda.

Nutrition Facts	
Serving Size 3 cubes	
Servings Per Recipe 8	
Amount Per Serving	
Calories 75	
Total Fat 1g	
Cholesterol 0mg	
Sodium 12mg	
Total Carbohydrate 19g	
Dietary Fiber less than 1g	
Sugars 17g	
Protein less than 1g	

Freshest Sugar-Free Lemonade

Sugar substitute to equal 1 cup (200 g) sugar
1 cup fresh lemon juice   250 ml
Lemon slices for garnish
Mint sprigs for garnish

1. Combine sugar substitute, lemon juice and 1 cup (250 ml) water in 2-quart (2 L) pitcher. Stir until sugar substitute dissolves.

2. Add 4 cups (1 L) water. Serve over ice and garnish with lemon slices and mint sprigs.

Nutrition Facts
Serving Size 1 cup (250 ml) Servings Per Recipe 6
Amount Per Serving
Calories 10
Total Fat 0g
Cholesterol 0mg
Sodium less than 1mg
Total Carbohydrate 9g
Dietary Fiber less than 1g
Sugars less than 1g
Protein less than 1g

Orange Tea Fizzy

5 - 6 (regular size) or 2 - 3 (family size)
decaffeinated tea bags
Sugar substitute to equal ½ cup (100 g) sugar
1 cup fresh orange juice   **250 ml**
3 cups diet lemon-lime soda   **750 ml**

1. Pour 3 cups (750 ml) boiling water over tea bags in large saucepan. Cover and let stand for 5 minutes. Remove tea bags. Add sugar substitute and stir until it dissolves.

2. Add orange juice and pour into 2-quart (2 L) pitcher with 2 cups (500 ml) ice cubes.

3. Just before serving, carefully pour soda down inside of pitcher.

Nutrition Facts
Serving Size 1 cup (250 ml) Servings Per Recipe 8
Amount Per Serving
Calories 15
Total Fat less than 1g
Cholesterol 0mg
Sodium 10mg
Total Carbohydrate 5g
Dietary Fiber less than 1g
Sugars 0g
Protein less than 1g

Sugar-Free Cocoa

¼ cup cocoa   20 g
Sugar substitute to equal 2 tablespoons
    (25 g) sugar
3¼ cups fat-free milk, divided   810 ml
½ teaspoon vanilla   2 ml
Ground cinnamon or nutmeg

1. Mix cocoa and sugar substitute
   in medium heavy saucepan.
   Add ½ cup (125 ml) milk,
   stirring constantly with whisk
   over medium heat until dry
   ingredients dissolve.

2. Gradually add remaining milk;
   cook and stir just until cocoa
   bubbles.

3. Remove from heat and stir in
   vanilla. Garnish with cinnamon or nutmeg.

Nutrition Facts	
Serving Size ¾ cup (175 ml) Servings Per Recipe 4	
Amount Per Serving	
Calories 79	
Total Fat less than 1g	
Cholesterol 4mg	
Sodium 89mg	
Total Carbohydrate 13g	
Dietary Fiber 2g	
Sugars 10g	
Protein 8g	

Holiday Cranberry Tea

10 whole cloves
1 stick cinnamon
2 cups reduced-calorie cranberry
    juice cocktail   500 ml
2 decaffeinated tea bags
Sugar substitute

1. Add cloves and cinnamon to
   1 cup (250 ml) boiling water
   in saucepan.

2. Reduce heat, cover and simmer
   for 10 minutes. Add 1 cup (250
   ml) water and cranberry juice and
   heat to boiling again.

3. Remove from heat, add tea bags
   and a little sugar substitute and
   cover. Let stand for 5 minutes.
   Remove spices and tea bags.

Nutrition Facts	
Serving Size 1 cup (250 ml) Servings Per Recipe 4	
Amount Per Serving	
Calories 28	
Total Fat 1g	
Cholesterol 0mg	
Sodium 25mg	
Total Carbohydrate 7g	
Dietary Fiber 1g	
Sugars 2g	
Protein 0g	

Soothing Orange Tea

Great stress reducer and relieves scratchy throats.

10 whole cloves
1 stick cinnamon, broken
2 cups reduced-sugar and calorie
   orange juice   **500 ml**
1 (family-size) or 2 (regular size)
   decaffeinated tea bags

1. Add cloves and cinnamon to 1 cup (250 ml) boiling water in saucepan.

2. Reduce heat, cover and simmer for 10 minutes. Add 1 cup (250 ml) water and orange juice and heat to boiling again.

3. Remove from heat, add tea bag(s) and cover. Let stand for 5 minutes. Remove tea bags and spices.

TIP: No sweetener needed with natural sweetness of orange juice.

Nutrition Facts
Serving Size 1 cup (250 ml) Servings Per Recipe 4
Amount Per Serving
Calories 25
Total Fat 0g
Cholesterol 0mg
Sodium 6mg
Total Carbohydrate 6g
Dietary Fiber 0g
Sugars less than 5g
Protein 0g

Berry-Banana Smoothie

1 cup reduced-fat vanilla yogurt	230 g
1 banana	
½ cup sliced fresh or frozen unsweetened strawberries	100 g
½ cup fresh or frozen unsweetened berries (mixed berries, blueberries or blackberries)	75 g

1. Combine all ingredients in blender. Process until smooth.

Nutrition Facts
Serving Size 1½ cups (375 ml) Servings Per Recipe 2
Amount Per Serving
Calories 153
Total Fat 1g
Cholesterol 2mg
Sodium 96mg
Total Carbohydrate 30g
Dietary Fiber 3g
Sugars 20g
Protein 8g

Cool Cranberry Refresher

4 decaffeinated green tea bags
1 mint tea bag
2 cups reduced-calorie cranberry juice
   cocktail, chilled   **500 ml**

1. Bring 3 cups (750 ml) water in medium saucepan to boiling. Remove from heat and add tea bags. Cover and let steep for 10 minutes. Remove and discard tea bags and refrigerate tea.

2. When tea is cold, add cranberry juice cocktail and stir. Serve over ice.

Nutrition Facts
Serving Size 1 cup (250 ml)
Servings Per Recipe 5
Amount Per Serving
Calories 19
Total Fat 0g
Cholesterol 0mg
Sodium 13mg
Total Carbohydrate 5g
Dietary Fiber 0g
Sugars 5g
Protein 0g

Cafe au Lait

2 cups fat-free milk, heated   **500 ml**
2 cups prepared strong decaffeinated
   coffee, hot   **500 ml**
Sugar substitute to equal 1½ tablespoons
   (22 ml) sugar

1. Combine milk, coffee and sugar substitute in bowl.

Nutrition Facts
Serving Size 1 cup (250 ml)
Servings Per Recipe 4
Amount Per Serving
Calories 51
Total Fat 0g
Cholesterol 2mg
Sodium 66mg
Total Carbohydrate 8g
Dietary Fiber 0g
Sugars 5g
Protein 4g

Summertime Iced Coffee

2 tablespoons decaffeinated instant
   coffee granules   10 g
1½ cups fat-free milk   375 ml
½ teaspoon vanilla   2 ml
Sugar substitute to equal 2 tablespoons
    (25 g) sugar
1 (16 ounce) bottle diet cola, cold   500 ml

1. Dissolve coffee crystals in ¼ cup (60 ml) hot water. Stir coffee granules, milk, vanilla and sugar substitute in large pitcher. Gently stir in cola. Serve over ice cubes.

Nutrition Facts	
Serving Size 1 cup (250 ml) Servings Per Recipe 3	
Amount Per Serving	
Calories 56	
Total Fat 0g	
Cholesterol 2mg	
Sodium 84mg	
Total Carbohydrate 8g	
Dietary Fiber 0g	
Sugars 6g	
Protein 4g	

Double Strawberry Smoothie

1 pint (2 cups) fresh strawberries   360 g
1 cup fat-free milk   250 ml
2 (6 ounce) cartons reduced-fat
    strawberry yogurt   2 (170 g)
½ cup crushed ice   125 ml

1. Wash and hull strawberries.

2. Add strawberries, milk, yogurt
    and ice to blender. Cover and
    process for about 30 seconds.

Nutrition Facts
Serving Size 1 cup (250 ml)
Servings Per Recipe 4
Amount Per Serving
Calories 96
Total Fat 0g
Cholesterol 3mg
Sodium 98mg
Total Carbohydrate 16g
Dietary Fiber 2g
Sugars 14g
Protein 8g

Breakfast
&
Brunch

Breakfast & Brunch Contents

Berry-Yogurt-Granola Bowl

½ cup fresh blueberries   75 g
½ cup sliced fresh strawberries   85 g
1 (6 ounce) carton low-carb strawberry yogurt,
    divided   170 g
¼ cup high-fiber, high-protein granola cereal,
    divided   20 g

1. Combine blueberries and
   strawberries in bowl and place
   half fruit mixture in each of
   2 cereal bowls. Top fruit with
   half yogurt. Top each with
   half granola.

Nutrition Facts	
Serving Size 1 bowl Servings Per Recipe 2	
Amount Per Serving	
Calories 191	
Total Fat 3g	
Cholesterol 8mg	
Sodium 145mg	
Total Carbohydrate 28g	
Dietary Fiber 7g	
Sugars 14g	
Protein 10g	

Cantaloupe Fruit Bowl

2 small cantaloupes
1 cup honeydew melon balls   180 g
1 cup fresh blueberries   150 g

1. Halve cantaloupes and remove seeds with spoon. With melon baller, scoop balls from inside cantaloupe.

2. Arrange cantaloupe balls and honeydew balls in 4 cantaloupe halves. Sprinkle tops with blueberries.

3. Serve within 1 to 2 hours for best results.

Nutrition Facts
Serving Size ½ cantaloupe with fruit
Servings Per Recipe 4
Amount Per Serving
Calories 75
Total Fat 0g
Cholesterol 0mg
Sodium 26mg
Total Carbohydrate 19g
Dietary Fiber 2g
Sugars 16g
Protein 2g

Rosy Morning Grapefruit

2 large pink grapefruit, halved
2 tablespoons reduced-fat buttery spread   30 g
½ teaspoon ground cinnamon   2 ml
Sugar substitute to equal 2 teaspoons (10 ml) sugar

1. Section each grapefruit half with grapefruit knife or paring knife by cutting around each section close to membrane. Sections should be loosened from shell completely.

2. Melt spread in bowl in microwave on HIGH for 10 seconds. Add cinnamon and sugar substitute and mix well. Drizzle over grapefruit halves.

3. Broil grapefruit halves in shallow baking pan about 4 inches (10 cm) from heat until tops bubble and are light brown.

Nutrition Facts	
Serving Size 1 grapefruit half Servings Per Recipe 4	
Amount Per Serving	
Calories 92	
Total Fat 5g	
Cholesterol 0mg	
Sodium 45mg	
Total Carbohydrate 13g	
Dietary Fiber 2g	
Sugars 8g	
Protein less than 1g	

Bell Pepper-Zucchini Frittata

A frittata is a baked flat omelet with vegetables and herbs.

1 cup frozen pepper stir-fry vegetables (red, green, yellow bell peppers and onions)	145 g
1 medium zucchini, shredded	
1 cup liquid egg substitute	245 g
¼ teaspoon crushed dried basil	1 ml

1. Preheat oven to 350° (175° C).

2. Cook and stir peppers in sprayed 10-inch (25 cm) skillet until water evaporates. Stir in zucchini and cook an additional 1 minute. Drain in strainer.

3. Combine peppers, zucchini, egg substitute and basil in bowl and pour into sprayed 9-inch (23 cm) pie pan. Bake for 25 minutes or until frittata sets and edges begin to brown.

4. Loosen frittata with knife around edges. Turn out onto plate and cut into four wedges. Serve hot or at room temperature.

Nutrition Facts
Serving Size ¼ frittata
Servings Per Recipe 4
Amount Per Serving
Calories 45
Total Fat 0g
Cholesterol 0mg
Sodium 125mg
Total Carbohydrate 4g
Dietary Fiber 1g
Sugars 2g
Protein less than 7g

Hearty Ham and Rice Scramble

This recipe is an excellent way to use leftover rice.

2 cups frozen seasoning blend (celery, onion, peppers, parsley)	285 g
8 slices 98% fat-free deli ham, diced	
2 cups cooked long grain white or brown rice	315 g/390 g
½ cup liquid egg substitute	120 g

1. Combine 1 to 2 tablespoons (15 to 30 ml) water and frozen seasoning blend in non-stick skillet over medium heat. Cook and stir until vegetables are tender, adding more water if needed. Continue cooking and stir until liquid evaporates.

2. Spray vegetables and skillet with nonstick cooking spray. Add ham and cook 1 to 2 minutes.

3. Stir in rice and mix well. Pour in egg substitute and continue to cook and stir until it sets.

Nutrition Facts
Serving Size ½ cup (125 ml)
Servings Per Recipe 6
Amount Per Serving
Calories 110
Total Fat less than 1g
Cholesterol 8mg
Sodium 200mg
Total Carbohydrate 18g
Dietary Fiber less than 1g
Sugars 2g
Protein 6g

Orange-Cream Cheese Quesadilla

2 tablespoons reduced-fat cream cheese   30 g
2 (8 inch) low-carb whole wheat tortillas   2 (20 cm)
1 tablespoon sugar-free orange marmalade   15 ml

1. Preheat oven or toaster oven to 400° (205° C).

2. Spread half cream cheese on each tortilla almost to edges. Spread half marmalade on top of cream cheese.

3. Fold each tortilla in half. Heat for 3 to 4 minutes or until cream cheese begins to melt.

Nutrition Facts
Serving Size 1 tortilla with filling Servings Per Recipe 2
Amount Per Serving
Calories 156
Total Fat 6g
Cholesterol 10mg
Sodium 390mg
Total Carbohydrate 21g
Dietary Fiber 11g
Sugars less than 1g
Protein 7g

Bacon, Egg and Cheese Tortilla

½ cup liquid egg substitute   120 g
2 (8 inch) low-carb whole wheat tortillas   2 (20 cm)
2 slices turkey bacon, cooked, crumbled
¼ cup finely shredded reduced-fat
     cheddar cheese   30 g

1. Scramble egg substitute according to package directions in sprayed skillet over medium heat.

2. Spread half scrambled eggs and half crumbled bacon on each tortilla. Sprinkle half cheese on each.

3. Roll and heat in microwave for 10 to 15 seconds.

Nutrition Facts
Serving Size 1 filled tortilla
Servings Per Recipe 2
Amount Per Serving
Calories 221
Total Fat 14g
Cholesterol 30mg
Sodium 757mg
Total Carbohydrate 8g
Dietary Fiber 3g
Sugars less than 1g
Protein 19g

Breakfast Toast Surprise

Sugar substitute to equal 1 tablespoon
    (15 ml) sugar
¼ teaspoon ground cinnamon   1 ml
2 slices sugar-free whole wheat bread
¼ cup part-skim ricotta cheese, divided   65 g

1. Preheat broiler.

2. Mix sugar substitute and cinnamon in small bowl and set aside.

3. Lightly toast bread, then spread each slice with half ricotta cheese. Sprinkle tops with cinnamon mixture.

4. Place toast under broiler for 1 to 2 minutes or until hot.

Nutrition Facts
Serving Size 1 slice toast
Servings Per Recipe 2
Amount Per Serving
Calories 67
Total Fat 1g
Cholesterol 1mg
Sodium 232mg
Total Carbohydrate 12g
Dietary Fiber 3g
Sugars 1g
Protein 6g

French Toast Sticks

4 slices sugar-free whole wheat bread
½ cup liquid egg substitute   120 g
Sugar substitute to equal 1 tablespoon
   (15 ml) sugar
½ tablespoon ground cinnamon   15 ml

1. Cut each slice bread into 3 pieces.

2. Pour egg substitute into shallow
    dish. In batches, coat bread sticks
    on both sides with egg substitute.

3. Cook each batch in sprayed 10-inch
    (25 cm) skillet on medium-high
    heat. Turn to brown each side.

4. Combine sugar substitute and
    cinnamon in small bowl. Sprinkle
    over warm toast.

Nutrition Facts
Serving Size 3 sticks
Servings Per Recipe 4
Amount Per Serving
Calories 85
Total Fat 1g
Cholesterol 0mg
Sodium 172mg
Total Carbohydrate 13g
Dietary Fiber 3g
Sugars less than 1g
Protein 6g

Cheesy Applesauce Muffin

1 whole wheat English muffin, halved
¼ cup reduced-fat small curd cottage cheese,
    well drained   55 g
½ cup unsweetened applesauce   130 g
½ - 1 teaspoon ground cinnamon   2 - 5 ml
Sugar substitute to equal 2 teaspoons
    (10 ml) sugar

1. Lightly toast muffin halves.

2. Top each with cottage cheese and applesauce

3. Combine cinnamon and sugar substitute in bowl. Sprinkle on applesauce.

4. Broil for 2 to 3 minutes until cheese and applesauce heat through.

Nutrition Facts	
Serving Size 1 muffin half	
Servings Per Recipe 2	
Amount Per Serving	
Calories 120	
Total Fat 1g	
Cholesterol 2mg	
Sodium 327mg	
Total Carbohydrate 22g	
Dietary Fiber 3g	
Sugars 9g	
Protein 7g	

Oven-Broiled Peaches

2 tablespoons reduced-fat buttery spread	30 g
1 tablespoon packed light brown sugar	15 ml
1 tablespoon frozen unsweetened apple juice concentrate	15 ml
½ teaspoon ground cinnamon	2 ml
2 fresh peaches, peeled, halved, pitted	

1. Preheat broiler.

2. Combine spread, brown sugar, apple juice concentrate and cinnamon in microwave-safe bowl. Microwave on HIGH for about 30 seconds and stir to combine. Set aside.

3. Use spoon to remove small amount of flesh from centers of peach halves. Turn peach halves upside down on sprayed broiler pan.

4. Spray and broil peaches 4 to 5 inches (10 to 13 cm) from broiler element for 4 minutes, keeping oven door open to check frequently. Remove from oven and turn right-side up.

5. Spoon cinnamon mixture evenly into peach centers. Broil 4 to 5 inches (10 to 13 cm) from broiler element. Keep oven door open and check peaches frequently until brown and bubbly.

Nutrition Facts
Serving Size 1 peach half
Servings Per Recipe 4
Amount Per Serving
Calories 38
Total Fat 0g
Cholesterol 0mg
Sodium 2mg
Total Carbohydrate 9g
Dietary Fiber 1g
Sugars 9g
Protein 0g

Scrambled Eggs with Tomatoes

1 tablespoon butter	15 ml
1 cup finely chopped onion	160 g
1 garlic clove, minced	
3 roma or pear tomatoes, seeded, diced	
1½ cups liquid egg substitute	365 g

1. Melt butter in non-stick 10-inch (25 cm) skillet over medium heat. Add onion and garlic, cook and stir until onion is tender. Add tomatoes.

2. Cover and simmer for about 10 minutes. Add eggs to skillet and cook and stir until eggs set but are still shiny and moist.

Nutrition Facts
Serving Size 1 cup (250 ml) Servings Per Recipe 4
Amount Per Serving
Calories 125
Total Fat 6g
Cholesterol 9mg
Sodium 169mg
Total Carbohydrate 6g
Dietary Fiber 1g
Sugars 3g
Protein 12g

Crispy Tortilla Scramble

¾ cup liquid egg substitute	185 g
¼ cup finely diced red bell pepper	40 g
2 tablespoons finely chopped parsley	8 g
2 teaspoons canola oil	10 ml
2 (6 inch) corn tortillas, halved, cut in ½-inch strips	2 (15 cm)/1.2 cm

1. Combine egg substitute, bell pepper, parsley and 2 tablespoons (30 ml) water in medium bowl.

2. Heat oil in non-stick 10-inch (25 cm) skillet over medium heat. Add tortilla strips and cook until crispy. Remove from skillet, drain and set aside.

3. Add egg mixture to skillet, cook and stir until eggs set but are still moist. Garnish eggs with crispy tortilla strips.

Nutrition Facts

Serving Size ½ cup (125 ml) egg with tortilla strips
Servings Per Recipe 2

Amount Per Serving
Calories 132
Total Fat 5g
Cholesterol 0mg
Sodium 184mg
Total Carbohydrate 11g
Dietary Fiber 2g
Sugars 1g
Protein 6g

Whole Wheat Crepes

½ cup egg substitute   120 g
1½ cups fat-free milk   375 ml
1 tablespoon canola oil   15 ml
¾ cup whole wheat flour   100 g

1. Whisk all ingredients in medium bowl until they mix well.

2. Preheat sprayed non-stick crepe pan or 10-inch (25 cm) skillet with sloping sides. When drops of water sizzle in pan, quickly pour in scant ¼ cup (60 ml) batter. Rotate pan so batter flows over entire surface.

3. When surface looks dry and edges brown, carefully turn crepe with spatula and cook other side just until it is light brown. Carefully remove crepe with spatula or invert skillet over wax or parchment paper so crepe will slide out. Place wax paper between crepes if not served immediately.

4. Spray skillet as needed and frequently stir batter before cooking.

5. Wrapped airtight, crepes can be refrigerated for 3 days or frozen for later use. Add your favorite filling and serve.

TIP: *This recipe will take some practice, so expect to use one recipe to learn how to use your skillet to make a perfect crepe. Your family and friends will really be impressed!*

Nutrition Facts	
Serving Size 2 crepes	
Servings Per Recipe 6	
Amount Per Serving	
Calories 102	
Total Fat 3g	
Cholesterol 0mg	
Sodium 15mg	
Total Carbohydrate 14g	
Dietary Fiber 2g	
Sugars 3 g	
Protein 5g	

Omelet for Two

½ cup egg substitute   120 g
2 teaspoons butter   10 ml

1. Combine egg substitute and 2 tablespoons (30 ml)
    water in small bowl. Beat with fork until it blends but
    is not frothy.

2. Melt butter in non-stick 8-inch
    (20 cm) skillet with flared sides
    over medium-high heat. Add egg
    mixture and lower heat to medium.

3. Stir gently until mixture has small
    pieces of cooked egg in liquid. Stop
    stirring and cook for an additional
    1 to 3 minutes or until egg mixture
    sets but is still shiny. Lift and fold
    omelet with spatula and transfer to
    warmed plate.

Nutrition Facts
Serving Size ½ omelet
Servings Per Recipe 2
Amount Per Serving
Calories 155
Total Fat 14g
Cholesterol 32mg
Sodium 113mg
Total Carbohydrate 1g
Dietary Fiber 0g
Sugars 1g
Protein 8g

Pizza Omelet

½ cup liquid egg substitute	120 g
2 teaspoons butter	30 g
2 tablespoons tomato-pizza sauce	30 g
3 tablespoons finely shredded reduced-fat	
mozzarella cheese	20 g

1. Combine egg substitute and 2 tablespoons (30 ml) water in small bowl. Beat with fork to combine but do not let mixture become frothy.

2. Melt butter in non-stick 8-inch (20 cm) skillet with flared sides over medium-high heat. Add egg mixture and lower heat to medium.

3. Stir gently until mixture has small pieces of cooked egg in liquid. Stop stirring and cook for an additional 1 to 3 minutes or until egg mixture sets but is still shiny.

4. Lift and fold omelet with wide spatula and transfer to warmed plate. Spoon pizza sauce over omelet and sprinkle with cheese.

Nutrition Facts
Serving Size ½ omelet
Servings Per Recipe 2
Amount Per Serving
Calories 171
Total Fat 13g
Cholesterol 33mg
Sodium 242mg
Total Carbohydrate 1g
Dietary Fiber 0g
Sugars 0g
Protein 13g

Cinnamon-Raisin French Toast

½ cup liquid egg substitute   120 g
½ cup fat-free milk   125 ml
½ teaspoon vanilla   2 ml
Sugar substitute to equal 2 teaspoons
      (10 ml) sugar
4 slices cinnamon-raisin bread

1. Beat egg substitute, milk, vanilla and sugar substitute in bowl until smooth. Pour into pie pan.

2. Heat sprayed 10-inch skillet over medium heat. Coat both sides of bread with egg mixture. Cook for about 4 minutes on each side or until brown.

Nutrition Facts

Serving Size 1 slice
Servings Per Recipe 4

Amount Per Serving

Calories 53

Total Fat 1g

Cholesterol 1mg

Sodium 103mg

Total Carbohydrate 7g

Dietary Fiber 1g

Sugars 3g

Protein 3g

Winter Fruit Compote

Delicious for breakfast or as a dessert.

1 Anjou pear with peel, diced
1 Granny Smith apple with peel, diced
¼ cup Craisins® or raisins   30 g/40 g
¼ cup frozen unsweetened apple juice
   concentrate   60 ml
½ teaspoon ground apple pie spice   2 ml
Sugar substitute to equal 1 tablespoon
   (15 ml) sugar

1. Preheat oven to 350° (175° C).

2. Combine pears, apples, Craisins® and juice concentrate in 9-inch (23 cm) square baking dish.

3. Combine apple pie spice and sugar substitute in bowl and toss with pear-apple mixture.

4. Bake for 25 minutes or until fruit is tender. Stir occasionally.

Nutrition Facts
Serving Size ½ cup (125 ml) Servings Per Recipe 4
Amount Per Serving
Calories 106
Total Fat 0g
Cholesterol 0mg
Sodium 8mg
Total Carbohydrate 27g
Dietary Fiber 3g
Sugars 16g
Protein 1g

Mushroom-Onion Omelet

2 tablespoons butter	30 g
½ cup chopped fresh mushrooms	35 g
¼ cup finely chopped onion	40 g
2 cups liquid egg substitute	245 g
½ cup fat-free milk	125 ml

1. Melt butter in non-stick 10-inch (25 cm) skillet with flared sides over medium-high heat. Add mushrooms and onion, cook and stir for about 4 to 5 minutes or until mushrooms and onion are tender. Remove and set aside.

2. Combine egg substitute and milk in bowl. Pour into skillet and cook over medium heat. When eggs begin to set, lift edges with spatula to allow uncooked eggs to flow underneath. Continue cooking until eggs set but are still moist.

3. Spread mushrooms and onions on one side of omelet. Carefully fold omelet in half and slide onto warmed serving dish.

Nutrition Facts
Serving Size ¾ cup (175 ml)
Servings Per Recipe 6
Amount Per Serving
Calories 83
Total Fat 4g
Cholesterol 44mg
Sodium 163mg
Total Carbohydrate 3g
Dietary Fiber 0g
Sugars 2g
Protein 5g

Tropical Breakfast Bagels

1 (3 inch) plain bagel	8 cm
1 banana, sliced	
1 (6 ounce) carton reduced-fat pina colada yogurt	170 g
1 tablespoon toasted coconut	15 ml

1. Split and toast bagel halves.

2. Combine banana and yogurt in bowl. Sprinkle with toasted coconut. Use as spread or spoon onto toasted bagel halves.

Nutrition Facts
Serving Size 1 bagel half
Servings Per Recipe 2
Amount Per Serving
Calories 235
Total Fat 4g
Cholesterol 5mg
Sodium 190mg
Total Carbohydrate 43g
Dietary Fiber 3g
Sugars 21g
Protein 8g

Breakfast Banana Sundae

A fun way to enjoy your breakfast!

1 cup reduced-fat small curd cottage cheese,	
divided	225 g
1 banana, sliced, divided	
2 tablespoons crushed pineapple in juice,	
drained, divided	30 g
2 maraschino cherries with stems, divided	

1. Evenly divide cottage cheese in 2 serving bowls. Top each with half banana slices, half pineapple and 1 cherry.

Nutrition Facts
Serving Size ½ recipe
Servings Per Recipe 2
Amount Per Serving
Calories 151
Total Fat 1g
Cholesterol 5mg
Sodium 476mg
Total Carbohydrate 21g
Dietary Fiber 2g
Sugars 14g
Protein 15g

Refreshing Mocha Smoothie

1 cup prepared strong decaffeinated coffee, frozen in ice cube trays	250 ml
1 (6 ounce) carton reduced-fat vanilla yogurt	170 g
⅓ cup fat-free milk	75 ml
1 teaspoon cocoa	5 ml
Sugar substitute to equal 3 teaspoons (15 ml) sugar	

1. Remove coffee ice cubes from freezer and let stand at room temperature for about 15 minutes to soften.

2. Place in blender with yogurt, milk, cocoa and sugar substitute. Blend until smooth.

Nutrition Facts

Serving Size ½ recipe
Servings Per Recipe 2

Amount Per Serving	
Calories 89	
Total Fat 1g	
Cholesterol 6mg	
Sodium 80mg	
Total Carbohydrate 14g	
Dietary Fiber 0g	
Sugars 14g	
Protein 18g	

Apple Cheese Muffins

1 English muffin, split	
1 tart apple, peeled, cored, chopped, divided	
¼ cup shredded reduced-fat cheddar cheese, divided	30 g

1. Preheat boiler.

2. Lightly toast muffin halves. Add half apple to each muffin half and sprinkle with half cheese. Broil just until cheese melts.

Nutrition Facts

Serving Size 1 muffin
Servings Per Recipe 2

Amount Per Serving	
Calories 142	
Total Fat 4g	
Cholesterol 10mg	
Sodium 224mg	
Total Carbohydrate 23	
Dietary Fiber 2g	
Sugars 9g	
Protein 6g	

Savory Cheese Strata

Delicious for brunch or supper.

2 slices reduced-fat wheat bread, cubed
½ cup liquid egg substitute   120 g
½ cup fat-free evaporated milk   125 ml
½ cup finely shredded reduced-fat sharp
    cheddar cheese, divided   60 g
4 drops hot red pepper sauce

1. Preheat oven to 325° (160° C).

2. Arrange bread cubes in sprayed 1½-quart (1.5 L) baking dish.

3. Combine egg substitute, evaporated milk, half cheese and hot pepper sauce.

4. Pour egg mixture over bread cubes, pushing cubes down into liquid. Let stand for 5 to 10 minutes and push cubes into liquid again. Sprinkle with remaining cheese.

5. Bake covered for 15 minutes. Remove cover and bake for 10 minutes or until puffy golden brown and knife inserted in center comes out clean.

Nutrition Facts	
Serving Size ¼ of strata	
Servings Per Recipe 4	
Amount Per Serving	
Calories 102	
Total Fat 3g	
Cholesterol 10mg	
Sodium 262mg	
Total Carbohydrate 9g	
Dietary Fiber 1g	
Sugars 5g	
Protein 10g	

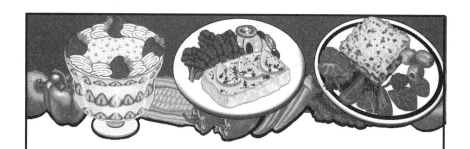

Soups,
Salads &
Dressings

Soups, Salads & Dressings Contents

Black Bean Soup

⅓ cup finely chopped onion   55 g
½ clove garlic, minced
¼ teaspoon dried oregano leaves   1 ml
1 (15 ounce) can black beans with liquid   425 g

1. Preheat sprayed 2-quart (2 L) saucepan over medium heat. Add chopped onion and garlic, cook and stir for 2 to 3 minutes. Stir in oregano and cook for 1 additional minute. Remove from heat.

2. Process beans with liquid in food processor or blender until desired consistency (chunky or smooth). For thinner soup, add small amount water.

3. Pour bean puree in saucepan with onion-garlic mixture. Heat until mixture boils, reduce heat and simmer for 10 minutes for flavors to blend.

Nutrition Facts
Serving Size ½ cup (125 ml)
Servings Per Recipe 4
Amount Per Serving
Calories 106
Total Fat less than 1g
Cholesterol 0mg
Sodium 422mg
Total Carbohydrate 20g
Dietary Fiber 8g
Sugars less than 1g
Protein 7g

Spicy Southwestern Soup

4 (14 ounce) cans 98% fat-free chicken broth	4 (400 g)
1 (10 ounce) can mild diced tomatoes and green chilies with liquid	280 g
2 teaspoons chili powder	10 ml
½ teaspoon ground cumin	2 ml

1. Combine all ingredients in large heavy saucepan.

2. Simmer for 30 minutes for flavors to blend.

Nutrition Facts
Serving Size 1 cup (250 ml)
Servings Per Recipe 8
Amount Per Serving
Calories 10
Total Fat less than 1g
Cholesterol 0mg
Sodium 204mg
Total Carbohydrate 1g
Dietary Fiber less than 1g
Sugars less than 1g
Protein 1g

Speedy Chicken Noodle Soup

1 (3 ounce) package chicken-flavored ramen noodles and flavor pack	85 g
2 (14 ounce) cans 98% fat-free chicken broth	2 (400 g)
1 cup frozen peas and carrots or mixed vegetables	140 g
1 cup cooked, cubed chicken breast	140 g

1. Prepare noodles according to package directions and set aside.

2. Heat chicken broth in large saucepan until it boils. Add vegetables and cook for 4 to 5 minutes.

3. Add chicken and noodles.

Nutrition Facts
Serving Size 1 cup (250 ml)
Servings Per Recipe 8
Amount Per Serving
Calories 94
Total Fat 3g
Cholesterol 15mg
Sodium 438mg
Total Carbohydrate 9g
Dietary Fiber less than 1g
Sugars 1g
Protein 8g

Easy Vegetable Soup

3 (14 ounce) cans 98% fat-free chicken broth   3 (400 g)
2 tablespoons chopped fresh parsley   10 g
1 (16 ounce) package frozen vegetables for
    soup mix (tomatoes, potatoes, corn,
    carrots, butter beans, okra, green beans,
    onions, celery)   455 g

1. Pour broth in large soup pot and heat until it boils.

2. Stir in parsley and frozen vegetables. Reduce heat and simmer for 15 to 20 minutes.

Nutrition Facts
Serving Size 1 cup (250 ml)
Servings Per Recipe 6
Amount Per Serving
Calories 45
Total Fat 0g
Cholesterol 0mg
Sodium 508mg
Total Carbohydrate 8g
Dietary Fiber less than 1g
Sugars 3g
Protein 3g

Cream of Asparagus Soup

1 pound fresh asparagus	455 g
1½ cups 98% fat-free chicken broth	375 ml
½ teaspoon onion powder	2 ml
1 cup fat-free milk	250 ml

1. Rinse and trim asparagus. Cook quickly in 2 cups (500 ml) boiling water in saucepan until tender. Drain, reserving 1 cup (250 ml) liquid.

2. Cut off and chop asparagus tips. Set aside for garnish. Stir reserved liquid, chicken broth and onion powder in 2-quart (2 L) saucepan. Bring to boiling and add remaining asparagus spears. Reduce heat and simmer for 5 minutes.

3. In batches, puree mixture in blender or food processor. Return to saucepan. Add milk and heat through. Sprinkle each serving with chopped asparagus tips.

Nutrition Facts
Serving Size 1 cup (250 ml)
Servings Per Recipe 4
Amount Per Serving
Calories 55
Total Fat 0g
Cholesterol 1mg
Sodium 267mg
Total Carbohydrate 9g
Dietary Fiber 2g
Sugars 6g
Protein 6g

Carrot-Ginger Soup

1 large yellow onion, halved, thinly sliced
3 cups grated carrots (3 medium carrots)   330 g
2 teaspoons freshly grated ginger root   10 ml
2 cups 98% fat-free chicken broth   500 ml

1. Add onion to sprayed 4 to 5-quart (4 to 5 L) soup
   pot. Cook and stir over medium heat for about
   3 to 4 minutes. Stir in carrots, ginger and
   2 to 3 tablespoons (30 to 45 ml) water. Continue
   cooking for 3 to 4 minutes.

2. Add broth and 2 cups (500 ml) water and bring
   to boiling. Cover and reduce heat. Simmer for
   30 minutes or until vegetables
   are very soft. Strain soup into
   large bowl; set aside vegetables
   and 1 cup (250 ml) liquid. Return
   remaining liquid to pot.

3. Add vegetables and 1 cup
   (250 ml) reserved soup to blender
   or food processor. Process until
   pureed. Stir puree into soup in
   pot and reheat.

Nutrition Facts
Serving Size 1 cup (250 ml)
Servings Per Recipe 4
Amount Per Serving
Calories 59
Total Fat less than 1g
Cholesterol 0mg
Sodium 344mg
Total Carbohydrate 12g
Dietary Fiber 3g
Sugars 6g
Protein 3g

Quick Tomato-Beef Soup

1 (14 ounce) can reduced-sodium beef broth   400 g
2 cups reduced-sodium tomato juice   500 ml
1 teaspoon Worcestershire sauce   5 ml
1 tablespoon fresh or ½ teaspoon
    crushed basil   15 ml/2 ml

1. Combine all ingredients in large saucepan and bring to boiling. Reduce heat. Cover and simmer 4 to 5 minutes. Serves 7.

Nutrition Facts
Serving size ½ cup Servings Per Recipe 7
Amount per Serving
Calories 18
Total Fat less than 0g
Cholesterol 0mg
Sodium 157mg
Total Carbohydrate 3g
Dietary Fiber 1g
Sugars 2g
Protein 1g

Savory Pumpkin Soup

1 cup coarsely chopped yellow onion	160 g
2 teaspoons curry powder	10 ml
⅛ teaspoon ground cumin	.5 ml
3 cups reduced-sodium 98% fat-free chicken broth	750 ml
2 cups canned pumpkin, solid pack	490 g

1. Combine onion, curry powder and cumin in sprayed 4 to 5-quart (4 to 5 L) soup pot. Cook and stir over low heat for 3 to 4 minutes.

2. Add chicken broth and stir in pumpkin and bring to a boil, reduce heat to low. Simmer for 25 to 30 minutes.

Nutrition Facts

Serving Size 1 cup (250 ml)
Servings Per Recipe 6

Amount Per Serving

Calories 48

Total Fat less than 1g

Cholesterol 0mg

Sodium 315mg

Total Carbohydrate 10g

Dietary Fiber 3g

Sugars 4g

Protein 3g

Apple-Celery Green Salad

6 cups torn green or red leaf lettuce	210 g
2 cups cored, coarsely chopped red apple with peels	250 g
1 cup sliced celery	100 g
2 - 3 tablespoons Green Salad Vinaigrette (page 135)	30 - 45 ml

1. Toss lettuce, apple and celery in salad bowl.

2. Drizzle Green Salad Vinaigrette over salad and lightly toss.

Nutrition Facts
Serving Size 1 cup (250 ml)
Servings Per Recipe 6
Amount Per Serving
Calories 57
Total Fat less than 1g
Cholesterol 0mg
Sodium 6mg
Total Carbohydrate 13g
Dietary Fiber 3g
Sugars 9g
Protein 2g

Orange-Red Onion Green Salad

2 large navel oranges, peeled, sliced	
8 thin red onion slices	
6 cups bite-size romaine or leaf lettuce	280 g
¼ cup Balsamic Vinaigrette (page 133)	60 ml

1. Quarter orange slices and place in salad bowl with red onion and lettuce.

2. Toss with Balsamic Vinaigrette.

Nutrition Facts
Serving Size 1 cup (250 ml)
Servings Per Recipe 6
Amount Per Serving
Calories 77
Total Fat 5g
Cholesterol 0mg
Sodium 6mg
Total Carbohydrate 11g
Dietary Fiber 3g
Sugars 7g
Protein 1g

Avocado-Grapefruit Salad

4 cups shredded romaine or leaf lettuce   190 g
1 avocado, peeled, seeded
1 grapefruit, peeled, sectioned
2 tablespoons Toasted Poppy Seed Fruit
    Dressing (page 138)   30 ml

1. On each of 4 salad plates, place one-fourth shredded lettuce.

2. Slice avocado in ¼-inch (6 mm) wedges. Arrange avocado wedges and grapefruit sections on lettuce.

3. Drizzle with dressing.

TIP: *One head of lettuce yields about 8 cups (280 g) shredded lettuce.*

Nutrition Facts
Serving Size 1 individual salad with dressing
Servings Per Recipe 4
Amount Per Serving
Calories 122
Total Fat 7g
Cholesterol 2mg
Sodium 35mg
Total Carbohydrate 14g
Dietary Fiber 5g
Sugars 6g
Protein 3g

5-Minute Italian Green Salad

1½ cups Italian mix giardiniera (cauliflower, carrots, celery, peppers and pickles in vinegar)	213 g
1 (10 ounce) package ready-to-eat romaine lettuce	280 g
3 tablespoons Classic Italian Dressing (page 137)	45 ml

1. Drain and rinse Italian mix vegetables in strainer to remove excess salt. Refrigerate remaining vegetables for later use.

2. Lightly toss lettuce and vegetables in salad bowl. Drizzle with dressing.

TIP: *Prepared ready-to-eat romaine lettuce will make this recipe a snap! In 1 (10 ounce/280 g) package of ready-to-eat romaine lettuce, there are 6 to 8 cups (1.4 to 1.9 L).*

Nutrition Facts
Serving Size 1 cup (250 ml) with dressing
Servings Per Recipe 6
Amount Per Serving
Calories 210
Total Fat 8g
Cholesterol 0mg
Sodium 369mg
Total Carbohydrate 3g
Dietary Fiber 1g
Sugars less than 1g
Protein less than 1g

Pear and Feta Cheese Salad

4 cups mixed field greens or bite-size romaine lettuce	170 g/190 g
2 Anjou pears, cored, cut in large chunks with peels	
2 tablespoons crumbled feta cheese	20 g
2 tablespoons Balsamic Vinaigrette (page 133)	30 ml
2 tablespoons chopped walnuts	15 g

1. On each of 4 salad plates, place one-fourth greens.

2. Arrange one-fourth pears over greens on each plate and sprinkle one-fourth feta cheese on each.

3. Drizzle with Balsamic Vinaigrette and garnish with walnuts.

Nutrition Facts
Serving Size ¼ recipe
Servings Per Recipe 4
Amount Per Serving
Calories 90
Total Fat 1g
Cholesterol 4mg
Sodium 62mg
Total Carbohydrate 21g
Dietary Fiber 3g
Sugars 15g
Protein 2g

Cottage Cheese Scramble

1 (16 ounce) carton reduced-fat small curd cottage cheese, drained	455 g
¼ cup chopped green or yellow bell pepper	40 g
½ cup chopped fresh tomato, drained	90 g
2 tablespoons chopped green onion with tops	15 g

1. Combine all ingredients in salad bowl.

TIP: Garnish with chopped parsley.

Nutrition Facts

Serving Size ½ cup (125 ml)
Servings Per Recipe 6

Amount Per Serving

Calories 85

Total Fat 1g

Cholesterol 4mg

Sodium 434mg

Total Carbohydrate 5g

  Dietary Fiber less than 1g

  Sugars 4g

Protein 14g

Baby Spinach-Pecan Salad

¼ cup chopped pecans	30 g
1 (6 ounce) package ready-to-eat baby spinach	170 g
2 tablespoons Honey-Mustard Dressing (page 140)	30 ml

1. Stir and toast pecans in small skillet over medium heat.

2. Drizzle spinach with dressing in salad bowl and toss lightly to coat.

3. Sprinkle salad with toasted pecans.

Nutrition Facts
Serving Size 1 cup (250 ml)
Servings Per Recipe 4
Amount Per Serving
Calories 137
Total Fat 14g
Cholesterol 0mg
Sodium 79mg
Total Carbohydrate 4g
Dietary Fiber 5g
Sugars 1g
Protein 3g

Warm Field Greens Salad

1 (10 ounce) package fresh mixed field greens	280 g
¼ cup chopped green onions with tops	25 g
2 egg whites, hard-boiled, chopped	
¼ cup Sweet-Sour Salad Dressing (page 134)	60 ml

1. Combine greens, green onions and egg whites in salad bowl.

2. Heat salad dressing in small saucepan until it boils. Immediately pour over salad and toss.

Nutrition Facts
Serving Size 1 cup (250 ml)
Servings Per Recipe 4
Amount Per Serving
Calories 86
Total Fat 7g
Cholesterol 0mg
Sodium 41mg
Total Carbohydrate 3g
Dietary Fiber 2g
Sugars 1g
Protein 3g

Overnight Layered Green Salad

1 head iceberg lettuce, shredded	
1 cup sliced celery	100 g
1 cup frozen green peas, partially thawed	145 g
¾ cup reduced-fat mayonnaise	170 g

1. Layer lettuce, celery and peas in large salad bowl.

2. Spread mayonnaise to cover and seal top of salad.

3. Cover tightly and refrigerate for several hours or overnight. Do not toss.

Nutrition Facts
Serving Size 1 cup (250 ml)
Servings Per Recipe 6
Amount Per Serving
Calories 110
Total Fat 9g
Cholesterol 9mg
Sodium 244mg
Total Carbohydrate 6g
Dietary Fiber 2g
Sugars 2g
Protein 2g

Creamy Coleslaw

6 cups shredded green cabbage	420 g
¼ cup chopped green bell pepper	40 g
¼ cup sliced green onions with tops	25 g
⅓ cup Creamy Slaw Dressing (page 134)	75 ml

1. Combine cabbage, bell pepper and green onion in salad bowl. Cover and refrigerate.

2. Just before serving, lightly toss cabbage mixture with dressing.

Nutrition Facts
Serving Size ¾ cup (175 ml)
Servings Per Recipe 8
Amount Per Serving
Calories 62
Total Fat 4g
Cholesterol 4mg
Sodium 92mg
Total Carbohydrate 7g
Dietary Fiber 2g
Sugars 2g
Protein less than 1g

Carrot-Pineapple Salad

3 carrots, peeled, coarsely grated
1 (8 ounce) can crushed pineapple, well
   drained   230 g
¼ cup chopped pecans   30 g
2 - 3 tablespoons reduced-fat mayonnaise   30 - 40 g

1. Combine all ingredients in salad bowl. Refrigerate until ready to serve.

Nutrition Facts	
Serving Size ½ cup (125 ml)	
Servings Per Recipe 6	
Amount Per Serving	
Calories 63	
Total Fat 3g	
Cholesterol 0mg	
Sodium 58mg	
Total Carbohydrate 8g	
Dietary Fiber 1g	
Sugars 5g	
Protein less than 1g	

Black Bean-Corn Salad

½ cup canned black beans, drained, rinsed   125 g
1 cup frozen corn kernels, thawed   165 g
½ cup diced tomatoes, drained   90 g
6 green onions with tops, sliced
Juice from 1 lime
Fresh chopped cilantro

1. Combine all ingredients except cilantro in salad bowl and refrigerate for at least 1 hour before serving. Garnish with cilantro.

Nutrition Facts	
Serving size ½ cup (125 ml)	
Servings Per Recipe 4	
Amount Per Serving	
Calories 66	
Total Fat 1g	
Cholesterol 0mg	
Sodium 67mg	
Total Carbohydrate 15g	
Dietary Fiber 3g	
Sugars 4g	
Protein 4g	

Fiesta Corn Salad

1⅓ cups frozen whole corn kernels	220 g
¼ cup chopped red bell pepper	40 g
½ cup chopped celery	50 g
¼ cup finely chopped onion	40 g
1 cup reduced-fat small curd cottage cheese, drained	225 g
⅓ cup reduced-fat sour cream	80 g

1. Prepare corn according to package instructions. Drain and cool.

2. Combine corn, red pepper, celery and onions in salad bowl. Add drained cottage cheese and strain mixture, if needed, to remove excess liquid. Stir in sour cream. Cover and refrigerate.

Nutrition Facts
Serving Size ½ cup (125 ml) Servings Per Recipe 6
Amount Per Serving
Calories 152
Total Fat 5g
Cholesterol 13mg
Sodium 338mg
Total Carbohydrate 18
Dietary Fiber 13g
Sugars 7g
Protein 31g

Crunchy Veggie Salad

½ cup sliced radishes	65 g
½ cup sliced celery	50 g
1 cup sliced cucumber	120 g
2 tablespoons Best French Dressing (page 132)	30 ml

1. Combine radishes, celery and cucumber in salad bowl. Refrigerate until ready to serve.

2. Drizzle salad with dressing and lightly toss.

Nutrition Facts
Serving Size ½ cup (125 ml)
Servings Per Recipe 4
Amount Per Serving
Calories 74
Total Fat 7g
Cholesterol 0mg
Sodium 24mg
Total Carbohydrate 2g
Dietary Fiber 1g
Sugars 1g
Protein 0g

Pea Salad with Tangy Basil Dressing

1 (16 ounce) package frozen petite peas, thawed	455 g
1 cup thinly sliced celery	100 g
¼ cup finely chopped green onions with tops	25 g
¼ cup Tangy Basil Dressing (page 135)	60 ml

1. Combine all ingredients in bowl. Refrigerate for at least 3 hours.

2. Drain excess dressing when ready to serve.

Nutrition Facts
Serving Size ½ cup (125 ml)
Servings Per Recipe 8
Amount Per Serving
Calories 107
Total Fat 7g
Cholesterol 0mg
Sodium 75mg
Total Carbohydrate 8g
Dietary Fiber 3g
Sugars 4g
Protein 3g

Warm Green Bean Salad

1 (16 ounce) package frozen whole green beans   455 g
1 (8 ounce) can sliced water chestnuts, drained,
    rinsed   230 g
¼ cup Sweet-Sour Salad Dressing (page 134)   60 ml
2 tablespoons bacon bits   15 g

1. Prepare green beans according to
    package directions. Plunge into
    ice water to stop cooking. Drain.

2. Combine green beans and water
    chestnuts in salad bowl.

3. Heat dressing in saucepan and
    pour over bean mixture.

4. Sprinkle bacon bits on top.

Nutrition Facts	
Serving Size ½ cup (125 ml) Servings Per Recipe 6	
Amount Per Serving	
Calories 119	
Total Fat 5g	
Cholesterol 0mg	
Sodium 52mg	
Total Carbohydrate 10g	
Dietary Fiber 3g	
Sugars 1g	
Protein 2g	

Tomato-Black Olive Salad

2 large tomatoes, cut into wedges
⅓ cup red onion slivers   55 g
8 large pitted black olives, sliced
2 tablespoons Feta Cheese Dressing (page 132)   30 ml

1. Combine tomatoes, red onions
    and olives in salad bowl and toss
    with dressing.

Nutrition Facts	
Serving Size ½ cup (125 ml) Servings Per Recipe 6	
Amount Per Serving	
Calories 66	
Total Fat 5g	
Cholesterol 0mg	
Sodium 55mg	
Total Carbohydrate 3g	
Dietary Fiber less than 1g	
Sugars less than 1g	
Protein less than 1g	

Italian Green Bean Salad

1 (16 ounce) package frozen cut Italian green beans or regular cut green beans	455 g
2 tablespoons diced pimento, drained	25 g
2 tablespoons grated parmesan cheese	15 g
⅓ cup Classic Italian Dressing (page 137)	75 ml

1. Cook green beans according to package directions and drain. Do not overcook.

2. Combine all ingredients in salad bowl. Refrigerate for at least 1 hour before serving.

TIP: Substitute 4 cups (540 g) canned cut Italian green beans, drained and rinsed, for frozen green beans.

Nutrition Facts	
Serving Size ½ cup (125 ml) Servings Per Recipe 8	
Amount Per Serving	
Calories 144	
Total Fat 14g	
Cholesterol 8mg	
Sodium 143mg	
Total Carbohydrate 7g	
Dietary Fiber 2g	
Sugars 2g	
Protein 1g	

Artichoke Red Pepper Salad

1 (6 ounce) jar marinated artichoke hearts   170 g
½ cup slivered red bell pepper   50 g
¼ cup slivered white or yellow onion   40 g
1 head torn romaine lettuce

1. Drain and coarsely chop artichoke hearts. Set aside 2 tablespoons (30 ml) marinade.

2. Combine artichokes, bell pepper, onion and set aside marinade in salad bowl. Toss with lettuce.

Nutrition Facts
Serving Size 1 cup (250 ml) Servings Per Recipe 8
Amount Per Serving
Calories 47
Total Fat 4g
Cholesterol 0mg
Sodium 78mg
Total Carbohydrate 4g
Dietary Fiber 1g
Sugars 1g
Protein less than 1g

Speedy Spanish Slaw

1 tablespoon canola oil	15 ml
1 tablespoon apple cider vinegar	15 ml
Sugar substitute to equal ½ teaspoon (2 ml) sugar	
3 cups ready-to-eat coleslaw mix	210 g
½ cup slivered bell pepper	50 g

1. Combine oil, vinegar and sugar substitute in bowl

2. Pour over coleslaw mix and bell pepper in salad bowl and gently toss.

3. Cover and refrigerate for at least 15 minutes before serving.

Nutrition Facts

Serving Size ½ cup (125 ml)
Servings Per Recipe 6

Amount Per Serving
Calories 31
Total Fat 3g
Cholesterol 0mg
Sodium 7mg
Total Carbohydrate 3g
Dietary Fiber 1g
Sugars 2g
Protein 1g

Broccoli Slaw-Tabbouleh Salad

1 (5.25 ounce) package tabbouleh wheat salad mix	150 g
1 tablespoon fresh lemon juice	15 ml
1 tablespoon olive oil	15 ml
2 cups packaged broccoli slaw mix (broccoli, carrots, red cabbage)	180 g

1. Combine dry tabbouleh mix and seasoning packet in large bowl. Add 1 cup (250 ml) boiling water and mix well. Cover and refrigerate for 30 minutes.

2. Add lemon juice and oil to tabbouleh. Set aside 1 cup (250 ml). Refrigerate remaining tabbouleh for later use or discard.

3. Combine set aside tabbouleh with broccoli slaw mix and toss.

Nutrition Facts
Serving Size ½ cup (125 ml)
Servings Per Recipe 8
Amount Per Serving
Calories 60
Total Fat 2g
Cholesterol 0mg
Sodium 125mg
Total Carbohydrate 11g
Dietary Fiber 3g
Sugars 1g
Protein 2g

Ramen Noodle-Chicken Slaw

1 (3 ounce) package ramen noodles, crushed
    (seasoning packet is not used)   85 g
½ cup diced cooked chicken breast   70 g
4 cups shredded cabbage or coleslaw mix   280 g
2 tablespoons Sesame Seed Dressing (page 133)   30 ml

1. Toast noodles in dry skillet over medium heat until they turn light brown. Stir constantly to avoid burning.

2. Combine toasted noodles, chicken and cabbage in salad bowl.

3. Drizzle with 2 tablespoons (30 ml) dressing. Toss lightly.

Nutrition Facts	
Serving Size ¾ cup (175 ml) Servings Per Recipe 8	
Amount Per Serving	
Calories 115	
Total Fat 8g	
Cholesterol 6mg	
Sodium 358mg	
Total Carbohydrate 8g	
Dietary Fiber 1g	
Sugars 1g	
Protein 4g	

Chicken-Macaroni Salad

1 (16 - 20 ounce) package frozen
    vegetable blend   455 - 570 g
1½ cups cooked reduced-carb macaroni   140 g
2 boneless skinless chicken breast halves,
    cooked, cubed
2 teaspoons Sesame Seed Dressing
    (page 133)   10 ml

1. Cook vegetables according to package directions and drain.

2. Combine all ingredients in salad bowl and lightly toss.

Nutrition Facts
Serving Size ½ cup (125 ml)
Servings Per Recipe 4
Amount Per Serving
Calories 279
Total Fat 7g
Cholesterol 43mg
Sodium 395mg
Total Carbohydrate 26g
Dietary Fiber 9g
Sugars 4g
Protein 26g

Tuna Waldorf Salad

1 (7 ounce) package solid white albacore tuna in water	200 g
2 tablespoons reduced-fat mayonnaise	30 g
1 red apple with peel, cored, diced	
½ cup diced celery	50 g
¼ cup chopped pecans	30 g

1. Drain tuna and break up with fork. Transfer to salad bowl.

2. Add mayonnaise, apple, celery and pecans. Toss lightly to mix.

Nutrition Facts
Serving Size ½ cup (125 ml) Servings Per Recipe 4
Amount Per Serving
Calories 86
Total Fat 2g
Cholesterol 19mg
Sodium 269mg
Total Carbohydrate 6g
Dietary Fiber 1g
Sugars 4g
Protein 11g

Curried Chicken and Fruit Salad

¼ teaspoon curry powder	1 ml
2 tablespoons reduced-fat mayonnaise, divided	30 g
2 cups diced cooked, boneless, skinless chicken breasts	280 g
1 cup seedless red or green grapes, halved	150 g

1. Combine curry powder and half mayonnaise in salad bowl.

2. Add chicken and grapes and stir. If needed to moisten ingredients, add remaining mayonnaise.

Nutrition Facts
Serving Size ½ cup (125 ml)
Servings Per Recipe 6
Amount Per Serving
Calories 224
Total Fat 6g
Cholesterol 82mg
Sodium 130mg
Total Carbohydrate 12g
Dietary Fiber 0g
Sugars 8g
Protein 30g

Tomato-Asparagus Salad

½ pound fresh asparagus   230 g
2 tomatoes, sliced
2 egg whites, cooked, chopped
2 tablespoons Classic Italian Dressing
    (page 137)   30 ml

1. Wash and trim asparagus spears. Cook asparagus in 1 inch (2.5 cm) boiling water for 5 minutes or until it is tender-crisp and drain.

2. Divide tomato slices evenly among 4 salad plates. Divide cooked asparagus spears and arrange on tomatoes. Sprinkle one-fourth cooked egg white on each salad and top with one-fourth Classic Italian Dressing.

Nutrition Facts
Serving Size 1 salad
Servings Per Recipe 4
Amount Per Serving
Calories 39
Total Fat less than 1g
Cholesterol 0mg
Sodium 122mg
Total Carbohydrate 6g
Dietary Fiber 2g
Sugars 3g
Protein 4g

Tuna Tomato Cups

3 large firm ripe tomatoes
1 (7 ounce) package solid white albacore tuna
    in water, drained   200 g
⅓ cup reduced-fat mayonnaise   75 g
½ cup chopped celery   50 g
1 tablespoon fresh lemon juice   15 ml
1 tablespoon finely chopped fresh parsley   15 ml

1. Cut off about one-third of stem end of each tomato. Carefully scoop out tomato flesh.

2. Combine tuna, mayonnaise, celery, lemon juice and parsley in bowl.

3. Mound one-third tuna mixture in each tomato cup.

Nutrition Facts
Serving Size 1 tomato cup
Servings Per Recipe 3
Amount Per Serving
Calories 182
Total Fat 10g
Cholesterol 34mg
Sodium 478mg
Total Carbohydrate 7g
Dietary Fiber 2g
Sugars 3g
Protein 16g

Shrimp Salad

4 cups shredded iceberg lettuce   310 g
1 large firm ripe tomato, cored, cut in wedges
½ pound frozen cooked shrimp, thawed   230 g
2 tablespoons Lemon-Oil Dressing (page 136)   30 ml

1. On each of 4 salad plates,
   arrange one-fourth lettuce.

2. Top with tomato wedges
   and shrimp.

3. Drizzle dressing on each.

Nutrition Facts
Serving Size 1½ cups (375 ml) Servings Per Recipe 4
Amount Per Serving
Calories 189
Total Fat 14g
Cholesterol 111mg
Sodium 313mg
Total Carbohydrate 2g
Dietary Fiber less than 1g
Sugars 2g
Protein 13g

Sprouts-Orange-Red Onion Salad

1 cup fresh alfalfa sprouts   35 g
2 large navel oranges, peeled, sliced
8 thin slices red onion
2 tablespoons Toasted Poppy Seed
    Fruit Dressing (page 138)   30 ml

1. Layer even amounts of sprouts, orange slices and red onion rings on 4 salad plates. Drizzle each salad with Toasted Poppy Seed Fruit Dressing.

Nutrition Facts
Serving Size 1 salad
Servings Per Recipe 4
Amount Per Serving
Calories 47
Total Fat 0g
Cholesterol 1mg
Sodium 9mg
Total Carbohydrate 11g
Dietary Fiber 2g
Sugars 7g
Protein 2g

Marinated Cucumbers

2 medium cucumbers, peeled, halved, seeded
½ cup Ranch-Style Buttermilk Dressing
    (page 139)   125 ml

1. Slice cucumbers and combine with dressing in shallow dish. Refrigerate for at least 4 hours. Drain before serving.

Nutrition Facts
Serving Size ¼ cup (60 ml)
Servings Per Recipe 8
Amount Per Serving
Calories 52
Total Fat 4g
Cholesterol 4mg
Sodium 78mg
Total Carbohydrate 5g
Dietary Fiber 0g
Sugars 2g
Protein 8g

Kidney Bean-Green Salad

2 cups shredded iceberg lettuce	155 g
½ cup canned kidney beans, rinsed, drained	130 g
½ cup sliced celery	50 g
½ cup diced tomatoes	90 g
2 tablespoons chopped red onion	20 g
¼ cup Balsamic Vinaigrette (page 133)	60 ml
1 egg white, hard-boiled, chopped	

1. Divide shredded lettuce evenly and arrange on 4 salad plates.

2. Combine kidney beans, celery, tomatoes and red onion in medium bowl. Toss with Balsamic Vinaigrette. Arrange mixture on top of lettuce. Sprinkle with chopped egg white.

Nutrition Facts	
Serving Size 1½ cups (375 ml) Servings Per Recipe 4	
Amount Per Serving	
Calories 101	
Total Fat 6g	
Cholesterol 0mg	
Sodium 106mg	
Total Carbohydrate 10g	
Dietary Fiber 3g	
Sugars 4g	
Protein 3g	

Red Cabbage Slaw

6 cups shredded red cabbage	420 g
½ cup finely chopped onion	80 g
½ cup reduced-fat mayonnaise	115 g
1 tablespoon white wine vinegar	15 ml

1. Combine cabbage and onions in large glass bowl.

2. In separate bowl, combine mayonnaise and vinegar. Pour mayonnaise mixture over cabbage and onions and toss.

TIP: You can also use about ⅓ cup (75 ml) Best French Dressing (page 132) to replace mayonnaise and white wine vinegar.

Nutrition Facts
Serving size ½ cup (125 ml)
Servings Per Recipe 12
Amount per Serving
Calories 57
Total Fat 3g
Cholesterol 4mg
Sodium 87mg
Total Carbohydrate 7g
Dietary Fiber 2g
Sugars 3g
Protein 1g

Boston Bibb Salad

4 cups bite-size pieces Boston bibb lettuce	220 g
1 (11 ounce) can mandarin oranges in juice, drained	315 g
¼ cup unsalted sunflower seed kernels, toasted	35 g
2 tablespoons Balsamic Vinaigrette (page 133)	30 ml

1. Combine lettuce, oranges and sunflower seeds in large bowl. Drizzle with dressing.

Nutrition Facts

Serving Size 1 cup (250 ml)
Servings Per Recipe 4

Amount Per Serving

Calories 83

Total Fat 7g

Cholesterol 0mg

Sodium 7mg

Total Carbohydrate 9g

Dietary Fiber 2g

Sugars 6g

Protein 3g

Pineapple-Apple Gelatin Salad

2 (.3 ounce) packages sugar-free mixed fruit gelatin mix	2 (10 g)
1 (20 ounce) can pineapple tidbits, drained, set aside juice	570 g
2 red apples with peels, cored, diced	
½ cup chopped pecans	55 g

1. Add gelatin to 2 cups (500 ml) boiling water in saucepan and stir until it dissolves.

2. Combine pineapple juice and enough water to equal 1 cup (250 ml). Stir into dissolved gelatin.

3. Pour mixture into 9 x 13-inch (23 x 33 cm) dish and refrigerate until it partially thickens.

4. Stir in pineapple, apples and pecans and refrigerate until gelatin sets.

Nutrition Facts
Serving Size ½ cup (125 ml)
Servings Per Recipe 12
Amount Per Serving
Calories 64
Total Fat 3g
Cholesterol 0mg
Sodium 33mg
Total Carbohydrate 9g
Dietary Fiber 1g
Sugars 7g
Protein less than 1g

Green Light Gelatin

1 (.3 ounce) package sugar-free lime gelatin mix   10 g
1 (8 ounce) can crushed pineapple in juice
       with liquid   230 g
2 tablespoons reduced-fat mayonnaise   30 g
1 cup low-fat small curd cottage cheese, drained   225 g

1. Add gelatin mix to 1 cup (250 ml) boiling water in saucepan and stir until it dissolves.

2. Stir in pineapple and juice, mayonnaise, and cottage cheese.

3. Pour into 1-quart (1 L) square dish and refrigerate until gelatin sets.

Nutrition Facts
Serving Size ½ cup (125 ml) Servings Per Recipe 6
Amount Per Serving
Calories 78
Total Fat 2g
Cholesterol 5mg
Sodium 227mg
Total Carbohydrate 7g
Dietary Fiber less than 1g
Sugars 5g
Protein 6g

Pineapple-Blueberry Gelatin Salad

2 (.3 ounce) packages sugar-free raspberry gelatin mix	2 (10 g)
1½ cups frozen blueberries, drained, set aside juice	235 g
1 (8 ounce) can crushed pineapple with juice, drained, set aside juice	230 g
1 (8 ounce) carton reduced-fat whipped topping, thawed	230 g

1. Add gelatin to 2 cups (500 ml) boiling water in saucepan and stir until it dissolves.

2. Combine blueberry juice, pineapple juice and enough water to equal 1 cup (250 ml) in large bowl. Stir into gelatin mixture. Set aside ½ cup (125 ml) gelatin mixture.

3. Add pineapple and blueberries to gelatin-juice mixture and mix well.

4. Pour into 9 x 13-inch (23 x 33 cm) dish. Refrigerate for several hours until gelatin sets.

5. Fold ½ cup (125 ml) reserved gelatin mixture into 1 cup (75 g) whipped topping. Lightly fold in remaining whipped topping. Spread over firm gelatin. Refrigerate before serving.

TIP: *One (15 ounce/425 g) can blueberries in light syrup with juice will also work in this recipe.*

Nutrition Facts
Serving Size ½ cup (125 ml)
Servings Per Recipe 16
Amount Per Serving
Calories 53
Total Fat 2g
Cholesterol 0mg
Sodium 25mg
Total Carbohydrate 7g
Dietary Fiber less than 1g
Sugars 5g
Protein less than 1g

Sunshine Gelatin Mold

2 (.3 ounce) packages sugar-free lemon gelatin mix	2 (10 g)
2 cups finely shredded green cabbage	140 g
1 cup grated carrot	110 g
1 cup chopped celery	100 g

1. Stir in gelatin into 2 cups (500 ml) boiling water in saucepan until it dissolves. Transfer to large bowl and refrigerate until it thickens, about 45 to 60 minutes.

2. Carefully fold remaining ingredients into thickened gelatin. Pour gelatin into sprayed 6-cup (1.4 L) ring mold.

3. Refrigerate until firm, about 4 hours or overnight. Remove gelatin salad from mold onto serving plate.

Nutrition Facts	
Serving Size ½ cup (125 ml)	
Servings Per Recipe 12	
Amount Per Serving	
Calories 9	
Total Fat less than 1g	
Cholesterol 0mg	
Sodium 21mg	
Total Carbohydrate 2g	
Dietary Fiber less than 1g	
Sugars less than 1g	
Protein less than 1g	

Peachy Fruit Salad

Doubles as a dessert!

2 (15 ounce) cans no sugar added sliced peaches in water, drained	2(425 g)
1 (20 ounce) can pineapple tidbits in juice, drained	570 g
1 (11 ounce) can mandarin oranges in light syrup, drained	310 g
2 (6 ounce) cartons nonfat reduced-sugar peach yogurt	2(170 g)

1. Cut peaches into chunks.

2. Combine with remaining ingredients in large bowl and fold together gently.

Nutrition Facts
Serving size ½ cup (125 ml)
Servings Per Recipe 12
Amount per Serving
Calories 56
Total Fat 0g
Cholesterol 0mg
Sodium 16mg
Total Carbohydrate 13g
Dietary Fiber 1g
Sugars 12g
Protein 1g

Peach Lover's Gelatin Salad

1 (3 ounce) package sugar-free peach gelatin mix	10 g
1 (15 ounce) can sliced peaches, set aside juice	425 g
1 (4 ounce) jar pureed peach baby food	115 g
¼ teaspoon almond extract	1 ml

1. Add gelatin to 1 cup (250 ml) boiling water in saucepan and stir until it dissolves.

2. Add juice from peaches and mix well. Stir in pureed peach baby food and sliced peaches and mix well.

3. Pour into 1½-quart (1.5 L) square dish.

4. Refrigerate for about 4 hours or until gelatin sets.

Nutrition Facts
Serving Size ½ cup (125 ml)
Servings Per Recipe 6
Amount Per Serving
Calories 75
Total Fat less than 1g
Cholesterol 0mg
Sodium 36mg
Total Carbohydrate 17g
Dietary Fiber 1g
Sugars 15g
Protein 1g

Best French Dressing

½ cup canola oil	125 ml
¼ cup red wine vinegar	60 ml
1 teaspoon dijon-style mustard	5 ml
1 teaspoon ground paprika	5 ml
Sugar substitute to equal 1 teaspoon (5 ml) sugar	

1. Combine all ingredients in shaker bottle with lid. Shake well to blend.

Nutrition Facts	
Serving Size 2 teaspoons (10 ml) Servings Per Recipe 18	
Amount Per Serving	
Calories 87	
Total Fat 9g	
Cholesterol 0mg	
Sodium 10mg	
Total Carbohydrate 0g	
Dietary Fiber 0g	
Sugars 0g	
Protein 0g	

Feta Cheese Dressing

2 tablespoons canola oil	30 ml
3 tablespoons red wine vinegar	45 ml
1 tablespoon fresh basil or 1 teaspoon dried basil	15 ml/5 ml
2 tablespoons crumbled feta cheese	20 g

1. Combine all ingredients in shaker bottle with lid. Shake well to blend.

Nutrition Facts	
Serving Size 1 tablespoon (15 ml) Servings Per Recipe 7	
Amount Per Serving	
Calories 41	
Total Fat 5g	
Cholesterol 2mg	
Sodium 13mg	
Total Carbohydrate 0g	
Dietary Fiber less than 1g	
Sugars 0g	
Protein less than 1g	

Balsamic Vinaigrette

2 tablespoons canola oil	30 ml
3 tablespoons dark or white balsamic vinegar	45 ml
¼ teaspoon dried basil, crushed	1 ml
¼ teaspoon dijon-style mustard	1 ml

1. Combine all ingredients with ¼ teaspoon (1 ml) pepper in shaker bottle with lid. Shake well.

2. Shake again before serving.

Nutrition Facts

Serving Size 1 tablespoon (15 ml)
Servings Per Recipe 5

Amount Per Serving	
Calories 55	
Total Fat 6g	
Cholesterol 0mg	
Sodium 1mg	
Total Carbohydrate 1g	
Dietary Fiber 0g	
Sugars 1g	
Protein 0g	

Sesame Seed Dressing

1 tablespoon toasted sesame seeds	15 ml
2 tablespoons canola oil	30 ml
2 tablespoons white wine vinegar	30 ml
1 tablespoon reduced-sodium soy sauce	15 ml

1. Combine all ingredients in shaker bottle with lid. Shake well to blend.

Nutrition Facts

Serving Size 2 teaspoons (10 ml)
Servings Per Recipe 7

Amount Per Serving	
Calories 45	
Total Fat 5g	
Cholesterol 0mg	
Sodium 83mg	
Total Carbohydrate less than 1g	
Dietary Fiber less than 1g	
Sugars less than 1g	
Protein less than 1g	

Sweet-Sour Salad Dressing

¼ cup canola oil	60 ml
¼ cup white wine vinegar	60 ml
Sugar substitute to equal 2 tablespoons (25 g) sugar	
¼ teaspoon Worcestershire sauce	1 ml

1. Combine all ingredients in shaker bottle with lid. Shake well to blend.

Nutrition Facts
Serving Size 1 tablespoon (15 ml)
Servings Per Recipe 8
Amount Per Serving
Calories 68
Total Fat 7g
Cholesterol 0mg
Sodium less than 2mg
Total Carbohydrate less than 1g
Dietary Fiber 0g
Sugars 0g
Protein 0g

Creamy Slaw Dressing

½ cup reduced-fat mayonnaise	115 g
Sugar substitute to equal 1 tablespoon (15 ml) sugar	
1 tablespoon cider vinegar	15 ml
½ teaspoon celery seed	2 ml

1. Combine all ingredients in bowl and refrigerate until serving time.

Nutrition Facts
Serving Size 2 teaspoons (10 ml)
Servings Per Recipe 12
Amount Per Serving
Calories 34
Total Fat 3g
Cholesterol 3mg
Sodium 60mg
Total Carbohydrate 2g
Dietary Fiber less than 1g
Sugars less than 1g
Protein less than 1g

Green Salad Vinaigrette

3 tablespoons canola oil   45 ml
2 tablespoons red wine vinegar   30 ml
Sugar substitute to equal 1½ teaspoons (7 ml) sugar

1. In bottle or jar with lid, combine oil, vinegar and sugar substitute in shaker bottle with lid. Shake well to blend.

Nutrition Facts
Serving Size 2 teaspoons (10 ml) Servings Per Recipe 6
Amount Per Serving
Calories 61
Total Fat 7g
Cholesterol 0mg
Sodium less than 1mg
Total Carbohydrate less than 1g
Dietary Fiber 0g
Sugars less than 1g
Protein 0g

Tangy Basil Dressing

¼ cup apple cider vinegar   60 ml
Sugar substitute to equal ¼ cup (50 g) sugar
¼ cup canola oil   60 ml
1 teaspoon crushed dried basil   5 ml

1. Combine all ingredients in shaker bottle with lid. Shake well to blend.

Nutrition Facts
Serving Size 2 teaspoons (10 ml) Servings Per Recipe 12
Amount Per Serving
Calories 41
Total Fat 5g
Cholesterol 0mg
Sodium less than 1mg
Total Carbohydrate less than 1g
Dietary Fiber 0g
Sugars less than 1g
Protein 0g

Lemon-Oil Dressing

¼ cup canola oil	60 ml
1 teaspoon grated lemon peel	5 ml
2 tablespoons lemon juice	30 ml
1 tablespoon chopped green onion with tops	15 ml
¼ teaspoon garlic powder	1 ml

1. Combine all ingredients in shaker bottle with lid. Shake well to blend.

Nutrition Facts

Serving Size 1 tablespoon (15 ml)
Servings Per Recipe 8

Amount Per Serving
Calories 61
Total Fat 7g
Cholesterol 0mg
Sodium 90mg
Total Carbohydrate less than 1g
Dietary Fiber less than 1g
Sugars less than 1g
Protein less than 1g

Classic Italian Dressing

¾ cup canola oil	175 ml
⅓ cup apple cider vinegar	75 ml
Sugar substitute to equal 2 teaspoons	
(10 ml) sugar	
½ teaspoon celery salt	2 ml
¼ teaspoon dry mustard	1 ml
¼ teaspoon dry cayenne	1 ml
¼ teaspoon garlic powder or 1 clove garlic,	
finely minced	1 ml

1. Combine all ingredients in tightly covered container and shake well.

Nutrition Facts
Serving Size 1 tablespoon (15 ml)
Servings Per Recipe 20
Amount Per Serving
Calories 70
Total Fat 8g
Cholesterol 0mg
Sodium 1mg
Total Carbohydrate 0g
Dietary Fiber 0g
Sugars 0g
Protein 0g

Toasted Poppy Seed Fruit Dressing

Perfect with Avocado-Grapefruit Salad (page 101).

2 teaspoons poppy seeds	10 ml
½ cup reduced-fat buttermilk	125 ml
½ cup fat-free sour cream	120 g
Sugar substitute to equal 1 tablespoon (15 ml) sugar	
1 tablespoon fresh lemon juice	15 ml

1. Toast poppy seeds in dry skillet over medium heat. Shake frequently and cook until seeds become fragrant. Set aside.

2. Combine buttermilk, sour cream, sugar substitute and lemon juice in bowl. Add toasted poppy seeds.

Nutrition Facts
Serving Size 1 tablespoon (15 ml)
Servings Per Recipe 16
Amount Per Serving
Calories 9
Total Fat 0g
Cholesterol 1mg
Sodium 15mg
Total Carbohydrate 1g
Dietary Fiber 0g
Sugars 0g
Protein 1g

Ranch-Style Buttermilk Dressing

¾ cup reduced-fat mayonnaise	170 g
½ cup reduced-fat buttermilk	125 ml
¼ teaspoon garlic powder	1 ml
¼ teaspoon onion powder	1 ml
1 tablespoon finely chopped fresh parsley	15 ml

1. Combine all ingredients in bowl until they blend well. Cover and refrigerate for at least 2 hours.

Nutrition Facts
Serving Size 1 tablespoon (15 ml)
Servings Per Recipe 20
Amount Per Serving
Calories 41
Total Fat 4g
Cholesterol 4mg
Sodium 76mg
Total Carbohydrate 2g
Dietary Fiber 0g
Sugars 1g
Protein 0g

Honey-Mustard Dressing

¼ cup canola oil	60 ml
3 tablespoons cider vinegar	45 ml
1½ tablespoons dijon-style mustard	22 ml
2 teaspoons honey	10 ml

1. Combine all ingredients in bowl and mix well.

Nutrition Facts

Serving Size 1 tablespoon (15 ml)
Servings Per Recipe 8

Amount Per Serving
Calories 68
Total Fat 7g
Cholesterol 0mg
Sodium 68mg
Total Carbohydrate 1g
Dietary Fiber 0g
Sugars 1g
Protein 0g

Soy Sauce Dressing

4 teaspoons canola oil	20 ml
4 teaspoons white wine vinegar	20 ml
2 teaspoons reduced-sodium soy sauce	10 ml
Sugar substitute to equal 1 teaspoon (5 ml) sugar	

1. Combine all ingredients in shaker bottle with lid. Shake well.

Nutrition Facts

Serving Size about 1 teaspoon (5 ml)
Servings Per Recipe 9

Amount Per Serving
Calories 19
Total Fat 2g
Cholesterol 0mg
Sodium 43mg
Total Carbohydrate less than 1g
Dietary Fiber 0g
Sugars less than 1g
Protein less than 1g

Vegetables
&
Side Dishes

Vegetables & Side Dishes Contents

Asparagus with Garlic

1½ pounds asparagus, washed, trimmed	680 g
2 cloves garlic, minced	
1 teaspoon dried crushed basil or	
1 tablespoon fresh basil, finely chopped	5 ml/15 ml
1 tablespoon reduced-sodium soy sauce	15 ml

1. Heat ⅓ cup (75 ml) water in 10-inch skillet until it boils.

2. Add asparagus, cover and cook over medium heat for about 5 minutes or until asparagus is tender-crisp. Uncover and continue to boil for about 1 to 2 minutes until water evaporates. Do not overcook. Remove asparagus and keep warm.

3. Combine garlic and basil in sprayed skillet. Cook and stir for 1 to 2 minutes.

4. Stir in soy sauce and pour sauce over cooked asparagus.

Nutrition Facts
Serving Size ½ cup (125 ml)
Servings Per Recipe 6
Amount Per Serving
Calories 26
Total Fat less than 1g
Cholesterol 0mg
Sodium 98mg
Total Carbohydrate 5g
Dietary Fiber 2g
Sugars 2g
Protein 3g

Oriental Asparagus

1 pound fresh asparagus	455 g
2 tablespoons reduced-sodium soy sauce	30 ml
Sugar substitute to equal 2 teaspoons (10 ml) sugar	
¼ teaspoon ground ginger	1 ml

1. Wash asparagus, remove tough ends and cut in 2-inch (5 cm) lengths. Add asparagus to 1 inch (2.5 cm) boiling water in 2-quart (2 L) saucepan. Cook until tender-crisp, about 4 to 5 minutes. Do not overcook. Drain and set aside.

2. Mix soy sauce, sugar substitute and ground ginger in bowl.

3. Combine asparagus and sauce in saucepan. Cook and stir over medium heat until sauce and asparagus heat through.

Nutrition Facts	
Serving Size ½ cup (125 ml)	
Servings Per Recipe 8	
Amount Per Serving	
Calories 17	
Total Fat less than 1g	
Cholesterol 0mg	
Sodium 156mg	
Total Carbohydrate 3g	
Dietary Fiber 1g	
Sugars 1g	
Protein 2g	

Beets in Sweet-Sour Sauce

1 (16 ounce) can sliced or whole beets	455 g
2 teaspoons cornstarch	10 ml
Sugar substitute to equal 2 tablespoons (25 g) sugar	
2 tablespoons cider vinegar	30 ml

1. Drain liquid from beets into measuring cup. Combine beet liquid and water to equal ½ cup (125 ml) and set aside.

2. Mix cornstarch and sugar substitute in bowl. Stir in vinegar and mix well.

3. Combine cornstarch mixture and beet liquid in saucepan over medium heat. Heat to boiling and boil for 1 to 2 minutes. Stir in beets and cook until they heat through.

Nutrition Facts
Serving Size ½ cup (125 ml) Servings Per Recipe 4
Amount Per Serving
Calories 31
Total Fat 0g
Cholesterol 0mg
Sodium 214mg
Total Carbohydrate 8g
Dietary Fiber 1g
Sugars 4g
Protein less than 1g

Mushroom-Broccoli Stir-Fry

1 pound fresh broccoli florets	455 g
1 (8 ounce) package fresh mushrooms, sliced	230 g
2 green onions with tops, sliced	
¼ cup slivered almonds, toasted	45 g

1. Stir-fry broccoli in sprayed wok or skillet on high heat.

2. Add 1 tablespoon (15 ml) water, cover and cook, stirring frequently until broccoli is tender-crisp. Add more water if needed. Remove broccoli and set aside.

3. Spray wok and add mushrooms and green onions. Cook and stir until liquid from mushrooms evaporates, about 3 minutes.

4. Return broccoli to wok, stir and heat mixture until hot. Sprinkle with almonds.

Nutrition Facts
Serving Size ¾ cup (175 ml)
Servings Per Recipe 6
Amount Per Serving
Calories 58
Total Fat 3g
Cholesterol 0mg
Sodium 18mg
Total Carbohydrate 5g
Dietary Fiber 2g
Sugars 2g
Protein 4g

Brussels Sprouts with Sour Cream

1 (10 ounce) package frozen brussels sprouts   280 g
1 onion, chopped
1 tomato, seeded, diced, drained
¼ cup reduced-fat sour cream, divided   60 g

1. Cook brussels sprouts according to package directions. Set aside and keep warm.

2. Cook and stir onion in sprayed skillet over medium heat until tender. Stir in tomato and brussels sprouts and cook until they heat through.

3. Garnish individual servings with 1 tablespoon (15 ml) sour cream.

Nutrition Facts
Serving Size ½ cup (125 ml)
Servings Per Recipe 4
Amount Per Serving
Calories 66
Total Fat 2g
Cholesterol 6mg
Sodium 16mg
Total Carbohydrate 10g
Dietary Fiber 3g
Sugars 2g
Protein 4g

Lemon-Garlic Brussels Sprouts

1 (10 ounce) package frozen brussels sprouts   280 g
1 clove garlic, finely minced
1 tablespoon fresh lemon juice   15 ml

1. Prepare brussels sprouts according to package directions. Drain and keep warm.

2. Cook and stir garlic in sprayed non-stick skillet over low heat for 1 to 2 minutes. Add drained brussels sprouts and lemon juice and stir for 2 to 3 minutes or until sprouts heat through.

Nutrition Facts
Serving Size ½ cup (125 ml)
Servings Per Recipe 4
Amount Per Serving
Calories 29
Total Fat 0g
Cholesterol 0mg
Sodium 28mg
Total Carbohydrate 6g
Dietary Fiber 3g
Sugars 0g
Protein 3g

Vegetable Patch Stir-Fry

1 large onion, thinly sliced
2 carrots, peeled, thinly sliced
1 - 2 cloves garlic, finely minced
1 small head (about 1¼ pounds) green cabbage,
    shredded   570 g
1 tablespoon reduced-sodium soy sauce   15 ml

1. Cook and stir onions, carrots and garlic in sprayed non-stick skillet or wok on medium-high heat until onions and carrots are tender.

2. Add shredded cabbage, soy sauce and 1 tablespoon (15 ml) water. Cook and stir for 4 minutes or until cabbage is tender-crisp.

Nutrition Facts
Serving Size ¾ cup (175 ml) Servings Per Recipe 6
Amount Per Serving
Calories 37
Total Fat 1g
Cholesterol 0mg
Sodium 111mg
Total Carbohydrate 9g
Dietary Fiber 3g
Sugars 5g
Protein 2g

Ratatouille

1 (1 pound) eggplant, peeled, cubed	455 g
1 (12 ounce) package frozen seasoning blend	
(celery, onions, peppers, parsley)	340 g
1 zucchini, sliced	
½ cup Easy Pasta Sauce (page 235)	125 ml

1. Combine eggplant, seasoning blend, zucchini and 2 tablespoons (30 ml) water in large heavy pan. Heat until mixture boils, then reduce heat to low and cover.

2. Cook for about 10 to 15 minutes or until vegetables are tender and drain.

3. Return eggplant mixture to pan. Add pasta sauce and stir until sauce heats through.

Nutrition Facts

Serving Size ½ cup (125 ml)
Servings Per Recipe 6

Amount Per Serving

Calories 34

Total Fat 0g

Cholesterol 0mg

Sodium 15mg

Total Carbohydrate 8g

Dietary Fiber 3g

Sugars 4g

Protein 1g

Eggplant-Tomato Casserole

1 (1 - 1¼ pound) eggplant, peeled, cubed	455 - 680 g
½ cup seasoned breadcrumbs, divided	60 g
½ cup liquid egg substitute	125 g
2 tomatoes, sliced	

1. Preheat oven to 350° (175° C).

2. Heat 2 inches (5 cm) water in saucepan until it boils. Add eggplant and cook until it is soft.

3. Drain and mash eggplant with fork. Stir in ¼ cup (30 g) breadcrumbs and egg substitute.

4. Spread eggplant mixture in sprayed 9-inch (23 cm) square baking dish and top with sliced tomatoes. Sprinkle tomatoes with remaining breadcrumbs and coat with cooking spray.

5. Bake for about 25 to 30 minutes or until tomatoes are tender and brown around edges.

TIP: *Over medium heat, cook and stir ⅓ cup (55 g) chopped onion and 2 minced garlic cloves in 8-inch (20 cm) skillet until onion is clear and tender. Stir into eggplant mixture.*

Nutrition Facts
Serving Size ½ cup (125 ml)
Servings Per Recipe 8
Amount Per Serving
Calories 50
Total Fat less than 1g
Cholesterol 1mg
Sodium 216mg
Total Carbohydrate 10g
Dietary Fiber 3g
Sugars 2g
Protein 3g

Green Beans and Water Chestnuts

1 (16 ounce) package frozen French-style cut
   green beans   455 g
½ cup sliced water chestnuts, rinsed, drained   75 g
¼ cup chopped green onion with tops   25 g
2 tablespoons reduced-sodium soy sauce   30 ml

1. Cook green beans according to package directions. Drain.

2. Transfer green beans to medium skillet or saucepan. Add water chestnuts, green onions and soy sauce and mix well. Cook and stir mixture over medium heat until hot.

Nutrition Facts
Serving Size ½ cup (125 ml)
Servings Per Recipe 6
Amount Per Serving
Calories 26
Total Fat 0g
Cholesterol 0mg
Sodium 174mg
Total Carbohydrate 5g
Dietary Fiber 2g
Sugars 2g
Protein 1g

Savory Green Beans

1 (16 ounce) package frozen cut green beans   455 g
1 onion, chopped
1 - 2 cloves garlic, finely minced
1 (14 ounce) can diced tomatoes seasoned with
    Italian herbs or other seasoning of choice   400 g

1. Cook green beans according to package directions. Drain and set aside.

2. Cook and stir onions and garlic in sprayed 10-inch (25 cm) skillet over medium heat for 5 to 6 minutes. Add a few drops water, if needed.

3. Pour tomatoes into onion mixture. Simmer for about 10 minutes.

4. Stir in green beans. Simmer until beans are hot.

Nutrition Facts
Serving Size ½ cup (125 ml) Servings Per Recipe 6
Amount Per Serving
Calories 53
Total Fat less than 1g
Cholesterol 0mg
Sodium 301mg
Total Carbohydrate 11g
Dietary Fiber 2g
Sugars 6g
Protein 2g

Citrus-Cumin Black Beans

Black beans never tasted so good!

1 (15 ounce) can black beans, drained, rinsed	425 g
½ teaspoon ground cumin	2 ml
1 tablespoon frozen orange juice concentrate	15 ml
1 cup chopped tomatoes	180 g
½ cup finely chopped red onion	80 g

1. Combine beans, cumin and orange juice concentrate in 1-quart (1 L) saucepan over low heat and heat for about 3 to 4 minutes or until hot.

2. When ready to serve, garnish each serving with chopped tomatoes and red onions.

Nutrition Facts
Serving Size ½ cup (125 ml) Servings Per Recipe 4
Amount Per Serving
Calories 63
Total Fat less than 1g
Cholesterol 0mg
Sodium 91mg
Total Carbohydrate 11g
Dietary Fiber 5g
Sugars 4g
Protein 2g

Sensational Stuffed Mushrooms

12 large mushrooms	
1 tablespoon finely chopped green onions with tops	15 ml
1 tablespoon reduced-fat cream cheese	15 ml
1 tablespoon finely chopped fresh parsley	15 ml
2 tablespoons plain or seasoned breadcrumbs	15 g

1. Preheat oven to 350° (175° C).

2. Remove stems from mushrooms and chop finely. Place caps on large sprayed baking pan.

3. Cook and stir chopped mushroom stems and green onions in sprayed skillet over medium heat for 2 to 3 minutes. Stir in cream cheese, parsley and breadcrumbs and cook and stir for 1 to 2 minutes.

4. Spoon cream cheese mixture evenly into mushroom caps and spray tops. Cover and bake for about 15 minutes until caps are tender. Uncover and bake for an additional 5 to 6 minutes or until tops brown.

Nutrition Facts
Serving Size 3 stuffed mushrooms
Servings Per Recipe 4
Amount Per Serving
Calories 37
Total Fat 2g
Cholesterol 3mg
Sodium 42mg
Total Carbohydrate 4g
Dietary Fiber less than 1g
Sugars 1g
Protein 3g

Green Chili, Okra and Tomatoes

1 (16 ounce) package sliced frozen okra, slightly thawed	455 g
1 tablespoon canola oil	15 ml
2 tablespoons chopped green chilies	30 g
2 (16 ounce) cans no-salt diced tomatoes with liquid	2 (455 g)
¼ teaspoon garlic powder	1 ml

1. Cook and stir okra in 2-quart (2 L) non-stick skillet over medium-high heat until excess liquid evaporates. When okra starts to stick, add oil. Continue to cook and stir constantly until okra becomes tender-crisp.

2. Stir in green chilies, tomatoes and garlic powder. Reduce heat to medium and cook, stirring frequently, for about 30 minutes.

TIP: *To prepare with fresh okra, heat oil in skillet over medium-high heat. Add okra and stir constantly until it is tender-crisp.*

Nutrition Facts
Serving Size ½ cup (125 ml)
Servings Per Recipe 8
Amount Per Serving
Calories 63
Total Fat less than 1g
Cholesterol 0mg
Sodium 91mg
Total Carbohydrate 11g
Dietary Fiber 5g
Sugars 4g
Protein 2g

Skinny Fried Okra

2 cups frozen sliced okra	200 g
½ teaspoon canola oil	2 ml
2 - 3 teaspoons cornmeal	10 - 15 ml
½ teaspoon dried basil, crushed	2 ml

1. Cover and cook frozen okra in 10-inch (25 cm) non-stick skillet over medium heat for 2 to 3 minutes or until ice melts. Uncover, cook and stir constantly until okra breaks apart.

2. Add oil and cook and stir until okra browns lightly and is tender.

3. Sprinkle with cornmeal and basil and stir for about 1 minute to mix well.

Nutrition Facts	
Serving Size ½ cup (125 ml)	
Servings Per Recipe 4	
Amount Per Serving	
Calories 46	
Total Fat less than 1g	
Cholesterol 0mg	
Sodium 3mg	
Total Carbohydrate 9g	
Dietary Fiber 3g	
Sugars 3g	
Protein 2g	

Veggie Pocket Sandwiches

4 cups shredded iceberg or romaine lettuce	310 g/190 g
½ cup chopped roma tomatoes, drained	90 g
½ cup chopped cucumber	60 g
2 tablespoons Ranch-Style Buttermilk Dressing (page 139)	30 ml
2 whole wheat pita breads, cut in half	

1. Lightly toss lettuce, tomatoes, cucumbers and Ranch-Style Buttermilk Dressing in salad bowl.

2. Open pita bread halves and spoon one-fourth mixture into each.

Nutrition Facts
Serving Size ½ pocket sandwich
Servings Per Recipe 4
Amount Per Serving
Calories 122
Total Fat 3g
Cholesterol 2mg
Sodium 217mg
Total Carbohydrate 22g
Dietary Fiber 4g
Sugars 3g
Protein 4g

Twice-Baked Potatoes

4 medium baking potatoes	
1 (8 ounce) package fat-free cream cheese	230 g
1 (8 ounce) carton fat-free sour cream	230 g
½ cup diced fresh tomato	90 g
¼ cup chopped red onion	40 g
¼ cup salsa	65 g

1. Preheat oven to 400° (205° C).

2. Arrange potatoes on shallow baking sheet. Prick skins with fork and bake for about 45 minutes or until potatoes are tender.

3. Cut potatoes in half lengthwise. Scoop out flesh and leave shells intact.

4. Mix potato with cream cheese and sour cream in bowl.

5. Mound potato filling in potato shells. Return potatoes to oven for 5 to 6 minutes. Garnish with tomato, onion and salsa.

Nutrition Facts

Serving Size 1 stuffed potato shell
Servings Per Recipe 8

Amount Per Serving

Calories 117

Total Fat 1g

Cholesterol 0mg

Sodium 256mg

Total Carbohydrate 20g

Dietary Fiber 14g

Sugars 2g

Protein 7g

Curried New Potatoes

1 pound small new (red) potatoes, scrubbed	455 g
1 teaspoon canola oil	5 ml
¼ teaspoon curry powder	1 ml
3 tablespoons chopped fresh parsley	10 g

1. Quarter potatoes and cut in 1-inch (2.5 cm) wedges. Pat dry with paper towels.

2. Heat oil in sprayed 10-inch (25 cm) skillet over medium-high heat and add potatoes. Turn potatoes to coat with oil. Cook and stir until potatoes brown and are tender. (Check for tenderness with fork. Skins should be crisp.)

3. Combine curry powder and parsley and sprinkle on potatoes. Heat and stir for 1 to 2 minutes.

Nutrition Facts
Serving Size ½ cup (125 ml)
Servings Per Recipe 4

Amount Per Serving

Calories 94

Total Fat 1g

Cholesterol 0mg

Sodium 8mg

Total Carbohydrate 19g

Dietary Fiber 2g

Sugars 1g

Protein 2g

Cinnamon-Maple Sweet Potatoes

3 medium sweet potatoes
3 teaspoons ground cinnamon   15 ml
2 tablespoons finely grated orange peel   10 g
3 tablespoons sugar-free maple syrup   45 ml

1. Scrub sweet potatoes and prick skins. Cover and cook in microwave on HIGH for 4 minutes on each side or just until potatoes are soft. Let stand for 1 to 2 minutes.

2. Scoop potato flesh from shells and mash with fork. Divide into 4 servings and sprinkle each with cinnamon and orange peel and drizzle with syrup.

Nutrition Facts
Serving Size ½ cup (125 ml)
Servings Per Recipe 4
Amount Per Serving
Calories 134
Total Fat less than 1g
Cholesterol 0mg
Sodium 36mg
Total Carbohydrate 31g
Dietary Fiber 2g
Sugars 2g
Protein 3g

Sweet Potato Souffle

2 large sweet potatoes, scrubbed, peeled, quartered
Sugar substitute to equal 3 tablespoons (35 g) sugar
2 tablespoons liquid egg whites   30 g
¼ cup fat-free evaporated milk   60 ml

1. Preheat oven to 325° (160° C).

2. Cut potatoes into pieces, place in saucepan and add water just to cover and bring to a boil.

3. Reduce heat to simmer, cover and cook for 10 to 15 minutes or until potatoes are very tender. Drain. Beat potatoes until smooth.

4. Add remaining ingredients and mix well. Spoon into sprayed 1-quart (1 L) baking dish. Bake for 25 minutes.

Nutrition Facts
Serving Size ½ cup (125 ml)
Servings Per Recipe 4
Amount Per Serving
Calories 66
Total Fat less than 0g
Cholesterol 0mg
Sodium 28mg
Total Carbohydrate 13g
Dietary Fiber 2g
Sugars 3g
Protein 2g

Crunchy Potato Cakes

1 cup mashed potato flakes	60 g
3 tablespoons reduced-fat sour cream	45 g
2 teaspoons canola oil	10 ml
1 cup crushed Corn Chex®	35 g

1. Prepare mashed potatoes with water according to package directions.

2. Stir sour cream into potatoes. Shape potato mixture into 3-inch (8 cm) cakes.

3. Preheat non-stick skillet with ½ teaspoon (2 ml) oil over medium-high heat. Coat 3 to 4 potato cakes on both sides with crushed cereal and place in hot skillet. Cook for about 3 to 4 minutes on each side.

Nutrition Facts
Serving Size 1 potato cake
Servings Per Recipe 8
Amount Per Serving
Calories 46
Total Fat 2g
Cholesterol 2mg
Sodium 28mg
Total Carbohydrate 7g
Dietary Fiber less than 1g
Sugars less than 1g
Prote5in 1g

Cheesy Squash Casserole

2 pounds yellow crookneck squash, thinly sliced	910 g
¾ cup shredded reduced-fat sharp cheddar cheese, divided	85 g
¼ cup reduced-fat mayonnaise	55 g
¼ cup liquid egg substitute	60 g

1. Preheat oven to 350° (175° C).

2. Add squash with water to cover into large saucepan. Bring to a boil. Reduce heat and cook for 8 to 10 minutes or just until squash is tender. Drain well in strainer and gently press out liquid with fingers.

3. Combine squash, ½ cup (60 g) cheese, mayonnaise and egg substitute in bowl.

4. Spoon into sprayed 2-quart (2 L) baking dish. Sprinkle with remaining cheese.

5. Bake for 30 minutes.

Nutrition Facts	
Serving Size ½ cup (125 ml)	
Servings Per Recipe 9	
Amount Per Serving	
Calories 106	
Total Fat 7g	
Cholesterol 16mg	
Sodium 213mg	
Total Carbohydrate 6g	
Dietary Fiber 1g	
Sugars 2g	
Protein 6g	

Parmesan Rice-Stuffed Squash

2 yellow crookneck squash, washed, trimmed	
1 cup cooked brown or white rice	195 g/160 g
2 tablespoons liquid egg substitute	30 ml
2 tablespoons finely grated parmesan cheese	13 g

1. Preheat oven to 350° (175° C).

2. Cut squash lengthwise and scoop out seeds with spoon.

3. Heat ½ inch (1.2 cm) water in 12-inch (32 cm) skillet until it boils. Place squash halves cut-side down in skillet, cover and simmer for 5 minutes. Turn squash halves cut-side up with slotted spoon and simmer for an additional 5 minutes or until squash is tender. Remove squash and drain on paper towels.

4. Combine rice and egg substitute in bowl.

5. Mound one-fourth rice mixture on each squash half. Sprinkle with one-fourth cheese and spray with non-stick cooking spray. Place squash halves on non-stick baking sheet.

6. Bake for 15 to 20 minutes or until cheese browns lightly.

Nutrition Facts
Serving Size 1 squash half
Servings Per Recipe 4
Amount Per Serving
Calories 87
Total Fat 1g
Cholesterol 2mg
Sodium 56mg
Total Carbohydrate 15g
Dietary Fiber 2g
Sugars 3g
Protein 4g

Feta Cheesy Spinach

1 (10 ounce) package frozen spinach	280 g
½ cup chopped onion	80 g
¼ cup reduced-fat cottage cheese	55 g
¼ cup crumbled feta cheese	35 g

1. Prepare spinach according to package directions. Drain. Squeeze spinach between paper towels to completely remove excess moisture.

2. Cook and stir onion in sprayed 10-inch (25 cm) skillet over medium heat until it is tender. Stir in spinach and cheeses, cook and stir over low heat until cheeses melt.

TIP: *Sprinkle each serving with toasted pine nuts.*

Nutrition Facts
Serving Size ½ cup (125 ml)
Servings Per Recipe 4
Amount Per Serving
Calories 72
Total Fat 3g
Cholesterol 11mg
Sodium 297mg
Total Carbohydrate 5g
Dietary Fiber 2g
Sugars 2g
Protein 6g

Summer Squash Scramble

⅓ cup chopped green or red bell pepper   50 g
⅓ cup chopped onion   55 g
1 garlic clove, minced
2 cups cubed yellow crookneck squash   225 g
Dash cayenne pepper

1. Preheat sprayed non-stick skillet over low heat.
    Add bell pepper, onion and garlic. Cook and stir
    for 3 to 4 minutes or until vegetables are tender.
    Remove from skillet and set aside.

2. Add squash and 2 to 3 tablespoons
    (30 to 45 ml) water to skillet.
    Simmer over medium heat, cover
    and cook for 8 to 10 minutes until
    water evaporates and squash is
    tender-crisp.

3. Add pepper-onion mixture and
    cayenne pepper. Cook and stir
    over medium heat until squash
    begins to brown.

Nutrition Facts	
Serving Size ½ cup (125 ml) Servings Per Recipe 4	
Amount Per Serving	
Calories 24	
Total Fat less than 1g	
Cholesterol 0mg	
Sodium 2mg	
Total Carbohydrate 5g	
Dietary Fiber 1g	
Sugars 3g	
Protein less than 1g	

Creamy Vegetable Medley

1 (16 ounce) frozen vegetable blend (such as broccoli, cauliflower, carrots)	455 g
1 tablespoon butter	15 ml
1 tablespoon all-purpose flour	15 ml
1¼ cups fat-free milk	310 g
Dash ground nutmeg	

1. Cook vegetables according to package instructions. Drain and keep warm.

2. Melt butter in saucepan over medium heat. Stir in flour with whisk and cook for about 2 minutes.

3. Add milk and nutmeg. Cook and stir until sauce thickens.

4. Spoon sauce over vegetables.

TIP: Add ½ cup (55 g) reduced-fat shredded Swiss cheese to thickened sauce.

Nutrition Facts
Serving Size ½ cup (125 ml)
Servings Per Recipe 6
Amount Per Serving
Calories 75
Total Fat 2g
Cholesterol 1mg
Sodium 76mg
Total Carbohydrate 10g
Dietary Fiber 2g
Sugars 5g
Protein 3g

Roasted Mixed Vegetables

2 pounds or more vegetables (asparagus, bell pepper, broccoli, eggplant, mushrooms, squash and/or onions)	910 g
¼ cup canola oil	60 ml
2 teaspoons crushed dried herbs (thyme, oregano, tarragon, rosemary or herb blend)	10 ml

1. Preheat oven to 400° (205° C).

2. Clean and trim vegetables. Heat 3 quarts (3 L) water in large saucepan until it boils. Blanch vegetables by adding to boiling water and cooking just until vegetables are barely tender.

3. Immediately immerse in cold water and drain on paper towels. Pat dry with paper towels.

4. Lightly toss vegetables with oil and herbs in roasting pan. Roast in oven for 5 to 6 minutes or until vegetables brown in spots.

Nutrition Facts
Serving Size ½ cup (125 ml)
Servings Per Recipe 8
Amount Per Serving
Calories 81
Total Fat 6g
Cholesterol 0mg
Sodium 18mg
Total Carbohydrate 5g
Dietary Fiber 2g
Sugars 2g
Protein 3g

Baked Tomato Halves

4 ripe, firm tomatoes, halved	
3 tablespoons grated parmesan cheese	20 g
1 cup Italian herb-seasoned breadcrumbs	120 g

1. Preheat oven to 375° (190° C).

2. Arrange tomatoes in shallow baking pan. Bake for 10 minutes.

3. Combine cheese and crumbs in bowl. Sprinkle crumb mixture over tomato halves.

4. Bake for 15 to 20 minutes or until topping browns.

Nutrition Facts
Serving Size 1 tomato half
Servings Per Recipe 8
Amount Per Serving
Calories 74
Total Fat 1g
Cholesterol 2mg
Sodium 429mg
Total Carbohydrate 13g
Dietary Fiber 1g
Sugars 2g
Protein 3g

Orange-Raisin Rice

½ cup brown rice	95 g
2 tablespoons raisins	20 g
½ cup coarsely chopped orange sections and juice	90 g

1. Cook brown rice according to package directions.

2. Stir in raisins and let stand for 5 minutes.

3. Just before serving, fold in orange sections and juice.

Nutrition Facts
Serving Size ½ cup (125 ml)
Servings Per Recipe 4
Amount Per Serving
Calories 65
Total Fat less than 1g
Cholesterol 0mg
Sodium 2mg
Total Carbohydrate 15g
Dietary Fiber 1g
Sugars 5g
Protein 1g

Ham-Veggie Fried Rice

1 cup frozen peas and carrots	140 g
½ cup cubed turkey ham	70 g
1 cup cooked brown rice	195 g
¼ cup liquid egg substitute	60 g

1. Cook and stir peas and carrots in sprayed 10-inch (25 cm) skillet over medium heat for 2 to 3 minutes or until they thaw. Drain any accumulated water.

2. Reduce heat to low, add ham and rice and heat for 3 to 4 minutes until ingredients heat through.

3. Push rice mixture aside and pour egg substitute in skillet. Cook until liquid sets and use spatula to turn. Do not stir. When egg substitute sets, mix gently with ham-rice mixture.

TIP: Serve with reduced-sodium soy sauce.

Nutrition Facts	
Serving Size ½ cup (125 ml)	
Servings Per Recipe 5	
Amount Per Serving	
Calories 93	
Total Fat 1g	
Cholesterol 16mg	
Sodium 298mg	
Total Carbohydrate 12g	
Dietary Fiber 2g	
Sugars 2g	
Protein 7g	

Mushroom-Rice Pilaf

1 (10 ounce) package frozen seasoning blend	
(onions, celery, peppers, parsley)	280 g
1 cup coarsely chopped fresh mushrooms	70 g
1½ cups 99% fat-free chicken broth	375 ml
½ cup brown rice	95 g

1. Add seasoning blend to sprayed saucepan. Cook and stir over medium heat until vegetables are tender. Add water if needed.

2. Add mushrooms, cook and stir for about 2 minutes.

3. Gradually add chicken broth and heat until mixture boils. Stir in brown rice.

4. Reduce heat, cover and simmer for about 50 minutes. Add more broth if needed.

Nutrition Facts
Serving Size ½ cup (125 ml)
Servings Per Recipe 6
Amount Per Serving
Calories 94
Total Fat 3.5g
Cholesterol 0mg
Sodium 261mg
Total Carbohydrate 19g
Dietary Fiber 1g
Sugars 3g
Protein 2g

Creamy Spinach with Walnuts

1 (16 ounce) package frozen leaf spinach	455 g
1 cup sliced fresh mushrooms	70 g
3 tablespoons reduced-fat whipped cream cheese	30 g
¼ cup chopped walnuts	35 g

1. Cook spinach according to package directions. Drain. Squeeze spinach between paper towels to completely remove excess moisture.

2. Cook and stir mushrooms in sprayed 10-inch (25 cm) skillet over medium heat until they are tender. Drain. Reduce heat to low, add spinach and cream cheese and cook and stir over low heat until cheese melts.

3. Divide into 5 servings and top each with walnuts.

Nutrition Facts
Serving Size ½ cup (125 ml)
Servings Per Recipe 5
Amount Per Serving
Calories 136
Total Fat less than 9g
Cholesterol 6mg
Sodium 143mg
Total Carbohydrate 9g
Dietary Fiber 5g
Sugars 2g
Protein 9g

Broccoli and Noodles

1 (16 ounce) package frozen broccoli florets	455 g
1 (3 ounce) package chicken-flavored ramen noodles with flavor pack	85 g
1 (10 ounce) can 99% fat-free cream of mushroom soup	280 g
½ cup sliced water chestnuts, drained, rinsed	70 g

1. Cook broccoli according to package instructions in 2-quart (2 L) saucepan. Do not overcook. Drain and set aside.

2. In same saucepan, cook noodles according to package instructions and add flavor pack. Stir in broccoli, soup and water chestnuts.

Nutrition Facts
Serving Size ½ cup (125 ml)
Servings Per Recipe 6
Amount Per Serving
Calories 102
Total Fat 3g
Cholesterol 2mg
Sodium 368mg
Total Carbohydrate 15g
Dietary Fiber 2g
Sugars 2g
Protein 3g

Broccoli-Cheese Mini-Pizza

1½ cups cooked frozen chopped broccoli, divided	280 g
2 whole wheat English muffins, split	
¾ cup Homemade Marinara Sauce (page 233)	175 ml
½ cup finely shredded part-skim mozzarella, divided	60 g

1. Drain cooked broccoli and spread on paper towels.

2. Lightly toast muffin halves. Spread each half with one-fourth Homemade Marinara Sauce, one-fourth broccoli and one-fourth cheese.

Nutrition Facts
Serving Size 1 muffin half
Servings Per Recipe 4
Amount Per Serving
Calories 145
Total Fat 3g
Cholesterol 9mg
Sodium 430mg
Total Carbohydrate 19g
Dietary Fiber 4g
Sugars 5g
Protein 6g

Green Chili-Cheese Spaghetti

1 (12 ounce) package reduced-carb spaghetti	340 g
1 (4 ounce) can chopped green chilies	115 g
1 (10 ounce) can 98% fat-free cream of mushroom soup	280 g
1½ - 2 cups shredded reduced-fat cheddar cheese, divided	170 - 230 g

1. Preheat oven to 350° (175° C).

2. Cook spaghetti according to package directions in large, heavy pan.

3. Drain spaghetti and return to pan. Stir in green chilies, soup and 1 cup (115 g) cheese.

4. Transfer spaghetti mixture to sprayed 9 x 13-inch (23 x 33 cm) baking dish. Sprinkle remaining cheese on top.

5. Bake for 25 to 30 minutes or until casserole bubbles and heats through.

Nutrition Facts
Serving Size ½ cup (125 ml)
Servings Per Recipe 16
Amount Per Serving
Calories 156
Total Fat 6g
Cholesterol 16mg
Sodium 294mg
Total Carbohydrate 13g
Dietary Fiber 5g
Sugars less than 1g
Protein 11g

Orange Asparagus Spears

1 pound fresh asparagus spears, trimmed	455 g
1½ tablespoons reduced-fat butter	22 ml
1½ tablespoons grated orange peel	22 ml
Juice of ½ orange	

1. Place asparagus in microwave-safe 2-quart (2 L) dish. Add 2 tablespoons (30 ml) water. Cover and cook on HIGH for 3 minutes. Rearrange spears and cook for an additional 3 minutes or until asparagus is tender-crisp.

2. Combine butter, orange peel and juice in 10-inch (25 cm) skillet over medium heat. Cook and stir until butter slightly browns. Add asparagus. Stir gently over low heat.

Nutrition Facts
Serving Size ½ cup (125 ml)
Servings Per Recipe 4
Amount Per Serving
Calories 73
Total Fat 5g
Cholesterol 0mg
Sodium 65mg
Total Carbohydrate 4g
Dietary Fiber 1g
Sugars 2g
Protein 3g

Granny Smith's Red Cabbage

1 medium onion, chopped
2 pounds red cabbage, shredded   910 g
2 Granny Smith apples, peeled, cored,
    thinly sliced
2 tablespoons red wine vinegar   30 ml
Sugar substitute to equal 1 tablespoon
    (15 ml) sugar
Dash cayenne pepper

1. Cook and stir onion in sprayed, large heavy pan until they become tender. Stir in cabbage, apples, vinegar, sugar substitute and cayenne pepper.

2. Cover and cook over low heat for 10 minutes. Add ½ cup (125 ml) water or more as needed.

Nutrition Facts	
Serving Size ½ cup (125 ml) Servings Per Recipe 8	
Amount Per Serving	
Calories 56	
Total Fat 0g	
Cholesterol 0mg	
Sodium 13mg	
Total Carbohydrate 13g	
Dietary Fiber 3g	
Sugars 11g	
Protein 2g	

Sauteed Mushrooms

1 tablespoon reduced-fat butter	15 ml
1 (8 ounce) packages sliced mushrooms	230 g
2 garlic cloves, finely minced	
¼ cup chopped fresh parsley	15 g

1. Melt butter in 10-inch (25 cm) skillet over medium heat. Add sliced mushrooms and cook and stir for about 5 to 7 minutes until they begin to brown.

2. Add garlic and parsley to skillet and cook and stir for 1 minute to cook garlic.

Nutrition Facts

Serving Size ½ cup (125 ml)
Servings Per Recipe 4

Amount Per Serving	
Calories 54	
Total Fat 4g	
Cholesterol 0mg	
Sodium 36mg	
Total Carbohydrate 3g	
Dietary Fiber 0g	
Sugars 2g	
Protein 3g	

Stir-Fry Snow Peas

1 teaspoon canola oil	5 ml
2 teaspoons peeled fresh ginger, minced	10 ml
1 pound package frozen snow peas, thawed, drained	455 g
½ teaspoon crushed dry basil leaves	2 ml

1. Heat oil in wok or 10-inch (25 cm) skillet over medium-high heat. Add ginger and stir-fry for 30 seconds. Do not burn. Add snow peas and toss with ginger.

2. Add basil and continue cooking and stirring for an additional 1 to 2 minutes or until snow peas are tender-crisp.

Nutrition Facts

Serving Size ½ cup (125 ml)
Servings Per Recipe 4

Amount Per Serving	
Calories 58	
Total Fat 1g	
Cholesterol 0mg	
Sodium 5mg	
Total Carbohydrate 8g	
Dietary Fiber 4g	
Sugars 0g	
Protein 3g	

Red Hot Onions

3 large red onions, thinly sliced	
½ - 1 teaspoon hot red pepper sauce	2 - 5 ml
1 tablespoon canola oil	15 ml
3 tablespoons red wine vinegar	45 ml

1. Place onions in large bowl. Pour 1 cup (250 ml) boiling water over onions and let stand for 1 minute. Drain.

2. Combine pepper sauce, oil and vinegar in bowl. Pour over onions. Cover and refrigerate for at least 3 hours. Drain before serving.

Nutrition Facts
Serving Size ¼ cup (60 ml) Servings Per Recipe 8
Amount Per Serving
Calories 38
Total Fat 1g
Cholesterol 0mg
Sodium 2mg
Total Carbohydrate 5g
Dietary Fiber 1g
Sugars 2g
Protein 0g

Main Dishes & Sauces

Main Dishes & Sauces Contents

No-Beans Beef Chili

1 onion, finely chopped	
1 (1 pound) package lean ground beef	455 g
1 (10 ounce) can mild diced tomatoes and green chilies	280 g
1 (1 ounce) packet reduced-sodium taco seasoning mix	30 g

1. Cook and stir onion in sprayed 10-inch (25 cm) skillet until tender. Do not brown. Remove and set aside.

2. In same skillet, cook and stir ground beef over medium heat until it browns. Transfer to strainer and drain. Wipe skillet with paper towels to remove excess fat.

3. Return meat and onion to skillet. Stir in tomatoes and green chilies, taco seasoning, and 2 cups (500 ml) water. Simmer for 25 to 30 minutes for flavors to blend.

Nutrition Facts
Serving Size ½ cup (125 ml) Servings Per Recipe 8
Amount Per Serving
Calories 131
Total Fat 6g
Cholesterol 36mg
Sodium 366mg
Total Carbohydrate 5g
Dietary Fiber less than 1g
Sugars 3g
Protein 13g

Oven-Barbecued Brisket

3 pounds lean brisket, fat trimmed off   1.4 kg
1 cup fat-free barbecue sauce   265 g

1. Preheat oven to 275° (140° C).

2. Seal brisket tightly in large piece of foil. Bake for
   2 hours 30 minutes in shallow baking pan (or
   1 hour per pound) and remove from oven to check for
   tenderness. When brisket is fork tender, drain meat
   juices and set aside. Brush barbecue sauce on brisket
   and reseal. Continue cooking for 20 to 30 minutes.

3. Remove brisket from oven. Transfer to separate
   dish, seal tightly and refrigerate. Refrigerate
   set aside meat juices in separate
   container. After juices cool, remove
   any congealed fat.

4. When ready to serve, preheat oven
   to 300° (150° C).

5. Slice cold brisket across grain of
   meat. Lay slices in 9 x 13-inch
   (23 x 33 cm) or smaller baking dish.
   Pour reserved liquid over brisket.

6. Cover and bake until meat is hot.

Nutrition Facts
Serving Size 1 slice (3 ounces/85 g) brisket
Servings Per Recipe 20
Amount Per Serving
Calories 178
Total Fat 6g
Cholesterol 59mg
Sodium 210mg
Total Carbohydrate 1g
Dietary Fiber 0g
Sugars 0g
Protein 28g

Easy Stuffed Peppers

3 large green bell peppers	
1 onion, finely chopped	
1 (1 pound) package lean ground beef	455 g
2 cups Homemade Marinara Sauce (page 233)	500 ml

1. Preheat oven to 350° (175° C).

2. Cut peppers lengthwise into 2 halves. Remove stems, seeds and white membrane.

3. Bring 4 cups (1 L) water in saucepan to a boil. Drop peppers into boiling water and boil for 5 to 6 minutes or until tender-crisp. Plunge into cold water and drain upside down on paper towels.

4. Cook and stir onion in sprayed 10-inch (25 cm) skillet over medium heat until tender. Remove from skillet and set aside.

5. Add ground beef to skillet, cook and stir until it browns. Drain meat in strainer and wipe skillet with paper towels to remove any excess fat.

6. In same skillet, combine ground beef, onion and one-half Homemade Marinara Sauce. Place pepper shells in sprayed 9 x 13-inch (23 x 33 cm) baking pan and mound mixture into peppers. Cover and bake for 20 minutes.

7. While peppers bake, heat remaining sauce in small saucepan.

8. Spoon sauce over baked peppers.

Nutrition Facts
Serving Size 1 stuffed pepper half with sauce
Servings Per Recipe 6
Amount Per Serving
Calories 247
Total Fat 16g
Cholesterol 52mg
Sodium 412mg
Total Carbohydrate 9g
Dietary Fiber 3g
Sugars 5g
Protein 16g

Stir-Fry Steak and Bok Choy

½ pound lean boneless flank or top sirloin steak, trimmed	230 g
1 head bok choy	
1 tablespoon canola oil, divided	15 ml
1 cup Stir-Fry Cooking Sauce (page 237)	250 ml

1. Slice steak into 1 x 3-inch (2.5 x 8 cm) thin strips and set aside.

2. Wash bok choy carefully and cut leaves from stems. Cut stems in ¼-inch (6 mm) slices and shred leaves.

3. Heat non-stick wok or 12-inch (32 cm) skillet over high heat. Add 1 teaspoon (5 ml) oil and bok choy stems. Cook, stirring constantly, for 1 to 2 minutes.

4. Add ¼ cup (60 ml) water, cover and cook for an additional 2 minutes. Add bok choy leaves and cook and stir for 1 to 2 minutes. Remove bok choy from wok.

5. Pour remaining oil into wok. When oil is hot, add steak. Cook and stir until meat browns slightly, about 3 to 4 minutes.

6. Stir in sauce and return bok choy to wok. Cook and stir until sauce boils and thickens.

Nutrition Facts

Serving Size 1 cup (250 ml)
Servings Per Recipe 4

Amount Per Serving

Calories 155

Total Fat 8g

Cholesterol 24mg

Sodium 185mg

Total Carbohydrate 5g

Dietary Fiber 1g

Sugars less than 1g

Protein 14g

Ground Beef Chili Stew

1 pound lean ground beef	455 g
2 medium onions, sliced	
2 garlic cloves, minced	
1 (14 ounce) can no-salt diced tomatoes	400 g
1 (14 ounce) can low-sodium beef broth	400 g
1 (4 ounce) can chopped green chilies and liquid	115 g
½ teaspoon cumin	2 ml
½ teaspoon chili powder	2 ml

1. Brown ground beef in large heavy pan over medium heat. Drain and discard grease. Set aside.

2. Add onions and garlic to pan. Cook and stir over medium heat for about 10 minutes. Pour in tomatoes, broth and green chilies. Bring to boil and add cumin, chili powder and ground beef. Reduce heat and simmer for about 15 minutes for flavors to blend.

Nutrition Facts	
Serving Size ¾ cup (175 ml)	
Servings Per Recipe 8	
Amount Per Serving	
Calories 145	
Total Fat 9g	
Cholesterol 5mg	
Sodium 28mg	
Total Carbohydrate 5g	
Dietary Fiber 1g	
Sugars 3g	
Protein 10g	

Chicken-Cream Cheese Rolls

4 small boneless, skinless chicken breast halves
¼ cup reduced-fat cream cheese   60 g
2 tablespoons chopped green onions with tops   15 g
4 slices turkey bacon

1. Preheat oven to 350° (175° C).

2. To thin chicken breasts, place in resealable plastic bag
   and pound with rolling pin until chicken breast is
   ¼-inch (6 mm) thick.

3. Combine cream cheese and
   green onions in bowl and
   spoon equal amount on each
   chicken breast. Roll chicken
   breast around cream cheese
   mixture. Wrap 1 slice bacon
   around each chicken roll and
   secure with toothpick.

4. Place in sprayed baking dish
   and bake for 30 minutes.

Nutrition Facts
Serving Size 1 roll
Servings Per Recipe 4
Amount Per Serving
Calories 164
Total Fat 8g
Cholesterol 69mg
Sodium 488mg
Total Carbohydrate less than 1g
Dietary Fiber 0g
Sugars less than 1g
Protein 23g

Lemon-Garlic Chicken

1 tablespoon fresh lemon juice	15 ml
1 tablespoon canola oil	15 ml
1 clove garlic, finely minced	
1 (2½ to 3 pound) whole chicken, cut into serving pieces	1.1 - 1.4 kg

1. Preheat oven to 350° (175° C).

2. Combine lemon juice, oil and garlic in small bowl.

3. In shallow baking dish, arrange chicken in single layer. Pour lemon juice mixture over chicken.

4. Cover and bake, basting occasionally, for about 45 minutes or until chicken is tender and juices run clear.

Nutrition Facts
Serving Size 1 piece chicken
Servings Per Recipe 8
Amount Per Serving
Calories 134
Total Fat 9g
Cholesterol 46mg
Sodium 135mg
Total Carbohydrate less than 1g
Dietary Fiber less than 1g
Sugars less than 1g
Protein 13g

Curried Chicken

1 (10 ounce) can 98% fat-free cream of mushroom soup	280 g
½ teaspoon curry powder	2 ml
4 boneless, skinless chicken breast halves, cooked, cubed	
⅓ cup slivered almonds, toasted	55 g

1. Combine soup, ½ soup can water and curry in 2-quart (2 L) saucepan.

2. Stir in cubed chicken, heat and stir until mixture heats through.

3. Sprinkle with almonds just before serving.

Nutrition Facts
Serving Size ⅔ cup (150 ml)
Servings Per Recipe 6
Amount Per Serving
Calories 185
Total Fat 7g
Cholesterol 59mg
Sodium 455mg
Total Carbohydrate 6g
Dietary Fiber 1g
Sugars 1g
Protein 25g

Oven-Fried Chicken

1 cup fat-free milk	250 ml
4 boneless, skinless chicken breast halves	
1 - 1½ cups whole wheat melba toast crumbs	120 - 180 g
1 tablespoon finely chopped parsley	15 ml

1. Soak chicken breasts in milk in bowl. Refrigerate for at least 30 minutes.

2. When ready to bake, preheat oven to 375° (190° C).

3. Combine toast crumbs and parsley in bowl. Drain chicken breasts and coat with crumbs, pressing crumbs lightly on both sides of chicken with fingers.

4. Arrange chicken on lightly sprayed baking sheet. Bake for 20 minutes and check for doneness by piercing chicken with knife. Chicken is done when meat is tender and juices run clear.

Nutrition Facts

Serving Size 1 chicken breast
Servings Per Recipe 4

Amount Per Serving
Calories 261
Total Fat 4g
Cholesterol 86mg
Sodium 594mg
Total Carbohydrate 17g
Dietary Fiber 1g
Sugars 3g
Protein 38g

Ginger-Lime Chicken

1 lime
⅓ cup reduced-sodium soy sauce   75 ml
½ teaspoon ground ginger   2 ml
4 small boneless, skinless chicken breast halves

1. Finely grate ½ teaspoon (2 ml) lime peel and squeeze 1 tablespoon (15 ml) lime juice.

2. Combine soy sauce, lime peel and juice, ginger, and 3 tablespoons (45 ml) water in 1-quart (1 L) saucepan. Boil mixture for 1 minute. Cool marinade to room temperature.

3. Pour cooled marinade over chicken breasts. Cover and refrigerate for several hours.

4. When ready to bake, preheat oven to 350° (175° C).

5. Pour off marinade and discard. Cover and bake chicken in sprayed baking dish for 45 minutes or until chicken is tender and juices run clear.

6. Uncover and brown chicken breasts under oven broiler for 5 minutes on each side.

Nutrition Facts
Serving Size 1 chicken breast half
Servings Per Recipe 4
Amount Per Serving
Calories 190
Total Fat 4g
Cholesterol 96mg
Sodium 228mg
Total Carbohydrate less than 1g
Dietary Fiber less than 1g
Sugars less than 1g
Protein 35g

Broccoli-Cheese Chicken

¼ cup slivered almonds	40 g
2 (10 ounce) packages frozen broccoli florets in cheese sauce	2 (280 g)
3 cups cooked, cubed chicken or turkey breast	420 g
¼ cup diced pimentos, drained	50 g

1. Cook and stir nuts in dry skillet over medium heat until they brown.

2. Cook frozen broccoli in sauce according to package directions.

3. Transfer to large saucepan and stir in chicken and pimentos.

4. Simmer, stirring constantly until chicken and broccoli mixture heats through. Add water if necessary to thin sauce.

5. Sprinkle with toasted nuts.

Nutrition Facts
Serving Size ⅔ cup (150 ml)
Servings Per Recipe 8
Amount Per Serving
Calories 147
Total Fat 5g
Cholesterol 40mg
Sodium 320mg
Total Carbohydrate 7g
Dietary Fiber 1g
Sugars 0g
Protein 18g

Stir-Fry Chicken Tenders

1 pound boneless, skinless chicken tenders	455 g
½ cup Stir-Fry Cooking Sauce (page 237)	125 ml
¼ cup sliced green onions with tops	25 g
1 (8 ounce) can pineapple chunks or tidbits, set aside juice	230 g

1. Place tenders and Stir-Fry Cooking Sauce in resealable plastic bag. Refrigerate and marinate for 15 to 20 minutes. Set aside marinade.

2. Preheat sprayed non-stick wok or skillet over high heat. Add about one-half chicken tenders and stir-fry for 2 minutes or until chicken browns. Repeat with remaining chicken. Set chicken aside and keep warm.

3. Add green onions, pineapple, 1 tablespoon (15 ml) pineapple juice and 1 to 2 teaspoons (5 to 10 ml) marinade to wok, cook and stir for about 1 minute. Discard remaining marinade.

4. Spoon onions and pineapple over chicken tenders.

Nutrition Facts

Serving Size 2 chicken tenders
Servings Per Recipe 4

Amount Per Serving
Calories 89
Total Fat 1g
Cholesterol 34mg
Sodium 54mg
Total Carbohydrate 6g
Dietary Fiber 1g
Sugars 5g
Protein 14g

Dee-Lish Chicken Spaghetti

1 (12 ounce) package reduced-carb spaghetti	340 g
1 (16 ounce) package reduced-fat Velveeta® cheese, cubed, divided	455 g
½ cup canned diced tomatoes and green chilies, drained, set aside liquid	120 g
2 cups cooked, cubed chicken	280 g

1. Preheat oven to 350° (175° C).

2. Prepare spaghetti according to package directions. Drain.

3. Set aside ¼ cup (30) cheese. Combine remaining cheese and tomatoes and green chilies in microwave-safe dish. Cover and heat on HIGH for 1½ minutes. Remove, stir and return to microwave for an additional 1½ minutes. Stir and let stand.

4. Combine cheese mixture with cooked spaghetti and chicken. If needed, add 1 tablespoon (15 ml) set aside tomato liquid.

5. Transfer to sprayed 9 x 13-inch (23 x 33 cm) baking dish and top with set aside cheese.

6. Cover and bake for about 25 to 30 minutes or until mixture bubbles and heats through.

Nutrition Facts	
Serving Size ½ cup (125 ml)	
Servings Per Recipe 12	
Amount Per Serving	
Calories 202	
Total Fat 4g	
Cholesterol 37mg	
Sodium 660mg	
Total Carbohydrate 18g	
Dietary Fiber 6g	
Sugars 3g	
Protein 20g	

Chicken and Dumplings

⅓ cup reduced-fat biscuit mix	40 g
¼ teaspoon crushed dried thyme	1 ml
2 (14 ounce) cans 98% fat-free chicken broth	2 (400 g)
1 (12 ounce) can 98% fat-free premium chicken breast in water	340 g

1. Stir baking mix and 3 tablespoons (45 ml) water to make soft dough. Add small amount biscuit mix if dough is too sticky. Add thyme.

2. Combine broth and chicken in 2-quart (2 L) saucepan and heat until mixture boils. Drop tablespoons of dumpling mixture onto boiling broth.

3. Reduce heat to medium (slow boil, not a simmer) and cook for 10 minutes. Cover and continue cooking for an additional 10 minutes.

Nutrition Facts

Serving Size 1 dumpling with chicken and broth
Servings Per Recipe 6

Amount Per Serving
Calories 77
Total Fat 1g
Cholesterol 21mg
Sodium 554mg
Total Carbohydrate 4g
Dietary Fiber 0g
Sugars less than 1g
Protein 11g

Chicken Italiano

¼ cup reduced-fat mayonnaise	55 g
4 boneless, skinless chicken breast halves, rinsed, patted dry	
¼ cup Italian seasoned breadcrumbs	30 g
¼ cup grated parmesan cheese	25 g

1. Preheat oven to 375° (190° C).

2. Lightly spread mayonnaise on both sides of each chicken breast. Combine breadcrumbs and cheese in flat dish.

3. Coat chicken with crumb mixture and transfer to foil-lined baking sheet.

4. Bake for 45 minutes or until chicken is tender and juices run clear.

Nutrition Facts
Serving Size 1 chicken breast half
Servings Per Recipe 4
Amount Per Serving
Calories 269
Total Fat 10g
Cholesterol 94mg
Sodium 684mg
Total Carbohydrate 7g
Dietary Fiber less than 1g
Sugars 1g
Protein 37g

Rosemary-Garlic Chicken

4 small boneless, skinless chicken breast halves
1 clove garlic, finely minced
2 teaspoons dried rosemary, crushed   10 ml
¼ to ½ cup 98% fat-free chicken broth   60 - 125 ml

1. Pat chicken dry with paper towels.

2. Brown chicken on both sides in sprayed non-stick skillet over medium-high heat. Reduce heat, add garlic and rosemary. Cook and stir for about 1 minute. Be careful not to burn garlic.

3. Add ¼ cup (60 ml) chicken broth to skillet and simmer gently for 30 minutes. Add remaining chicken broth as needed.

4. Chicken is done when juices run clear and chicken is tender.

TIP: *Replace rosemary with tarragon for a different flavor.*

Nutrition Facts	
Serving Size 1 chicken breast half	
Servings Per Recipe 4	
Amount Per Serving	
Calories 103	
Total Fat 2g	
Cholesterol 49mg	
Sodium 273mg	
Total Carbohydrate less than 1g	
Dietary Fiber less than 1g	
Sugars 0g	
Protein 20g	

Chicken and Wild Rice Supreme

1 (6 ounce) package reduced-sodium long grain-wild rice mix	170 g
2 large boneless, skinless chicken breast halves, cooked, cubed	
1 (10 ounce) can 98% fat-free cream of mushroom soup	280 g
1 (4 ounce) jar diced pimentos with liquid	115 g

1. Preheat oven to 350° (175° C).

2. Prepare rice according to package directions.

3. Combine all ingredients and ¼ cup (60 ml) water in bowl. Pour into sprayed 7 x 11-inch (18 x 28 cm) or 9-inch (23 cm) square baking dish.

4. Cover and bake for 25 minutes or until mixture bubbles and heats through.

Nutrition Facts
Serving Size 1 cup (250 ml)
Servings Per Recipe 8
Amount Per Serving
Calories 183
Total Fat 4g
Cholesterol 31mg
Sodium 424mg
Total Carbohydrate 22g
Dietary Fiber 1g
Sugars 1g
Protein 14g

Chicken with Sugar Snap Peas

1 (16 ounce) package frozen sugar snap peas   455 g
1 (8 ounce) package mushrooms, cleaned, sliced   230 g
2 large boneless, skinless chicken breast
    halves, cooked, cut into strips
⅓ cup Sweet-and-Sour Sauce (page 234)   75 ml

1. Cook sugar snap peas according to package directions. Immediately rinse in cool water to stop cooking, drain and set aside.

2. Cook and stir mushrooms in large sprayed skillet over medium heat for 5 to 6 minutes.

3. Add peas, chicken strips and Sweet-and-Sour Sauce; stir until mixture heats through.

TIP: *Speed preparation by using deli-cooked chicken.*

Nutrition Facts	
Serving Size 1 cup (250 ml) Servings Per Recipe 8	
Amount Per Serving	
Calories 79	
Total Fat 1g	
Cholesterol 21mg	
Sodium 168mg	
Total Carbohydrate 8g	
Dietary Fiber 2g	
Sugars 3g	
Protein 11g	

Low-Carb Chicken Fajitas

1 garlic clove, finely minced
1 cup sliced yellow or white onion   160 g
1 cup green or red bell pepper, cut into strips   90 g
1 large chicken breast half, cooked, cut into strips
1 teaspoon fajita seasoning   5 ml
4 low-carb whole wheat tortillas

1. Preheat oven to 300° (150° C).

2. Cook and stir garlic, onion and bell pepper in large sprayed skillet over medium heat until they are slightly brown and tender. Add chicken breast strips and fajita seasoning; simmer for 3 to 4 minutes.

3. Serve with warm tortillas.

Nutrition Facts	
Serving Size 1 fajita	
Servings Per Recipe 4	
Amount Per Serving	
Calories 160	
Total Fat 1g	
Cholesterol 17mg	
Sodium 232mg	
Total Carbohydrate 27g	
Dietary Fiber 3g	
Sugars 4g	
Protein 10g	

Chicken-Cheese Quesadillas

1½ cups frozen seasoning blend (onion,
    bell peppers, celery, parsley)   215 g
2 large boneless, skinless chicken breast
    halves, cooked, cut into strips
8 (8 inch) low carb whole wheat tortillas   8 (20 cm)
1 cup shredded reduced-fat cheddar cheese   115 g

1. Add seasoning blend to sprayed 10-inch (25 cm) skillet. Cook and stir over medium-high heat until tender. Add chicken strips, cook and stir for 3 to 4 minutes until strips become hot. Remove chicken mixture and wipe skillet with paper towels.

2. On each of 4 tortillas, spoon one-fourth chicken mixture. Top with cheese and cover with another tortilla.

3. Cook each quesadilla in sprayed skillet on both sides until tortillas brown, spraying with cooking spray as needed.

4. Cut each quesadilla into 4 wedges.

Nutrition Facts
Serving Size 2 wedges
Servings Per Recipe 8
Amount Per Serving
Calories 210
Total Fat 12g
Cholesterol 42mg
Sodium 561mg
Total Carbohydrate 8g
Dietary Fiber 3g
Sugars less than 1g
Protein 20g

Creamy Chicken Burrito

1 tablespoon reduced fat cream cheese	15 ml
1 (8 inch) low carb whole wheat tortilla	20 cm
1 - 2 tablespoons chopped cooked chicken breast	10 - 20 g
2 teaspoons chopped green onions with tops	10 ml
1 tablespoon salsa	15 ml

1. Preheat oven to 400° (205° C).

2. Spread cream cheese near edge of tortilla. Add chicken, green onion and salsa. Spray and roll tortilla. Place seam-side down onto sprayed baking sheet.

3. Bake for 5 to 6 minutes or until cream cheese melts.

Nutrition Facts
Serving Size 1 burrito
Servings Per Recipe 1
Amount Per Serving
Calories 160
Total Fat 5g
Cholesterol 16mg
Sodium 382mg
Total Carbohydrate 16g
Dietary Fiber 11g
Sugars less than 1g
Protein 9g

Easy Chicken Divan

3 cups fresh broccoli florets, steamed until
    tender-crisp, drained   215 g
2 boneless, skinless chicken breast halves,
    cooked, sliced
1 (10 ounce) can 98% fat-free cream of
    chicken soup   280 g
½ cup finely shredded reduced-fat
    cheddar cheese   60 g

1. Preheat oven to 375° (190° C).

2. Place broccoli florets in sprayed shallow baking dish.

3. Spread chicken slices on broccoli. Spoon soup evenly over chicken. Sprinkle with cheese and bake for 15 to 20 minutes until thoroughly heated.

Nutrition Facts
Serving Size 1½ cups (375 ml)
Servings Per Recipe 4
Amount Per Serving
Calories 180
Total Fat 7g
Cholesterol 54mg
Sodium 406mg
Total Carbohydrate 10g
Dietary Fiber 0g
Sugars 0g
Protein 20g

Mandarin Chicken Tenders

1½ - 2 pounds chicken tenders	680 - 910 g
1 cup orange juice	250 ml
2 teaspoons reduced-sodium soy sauce	10 ml
½ teaspoon ground ginger	2 ml
1 (11 ounce) can mandarin oranges, drained	315 g

1. Rinse chicken tenders and pat dry with paper towels.

2. Preheat sprayed 10-inch (25 cm) skillet over medium heat. Add half chicken tenders and cook until chicken is no longer pink and is light brown on both sides. Remove and set aside. Add remaining chicken tenders to skillet, spraying as needed. Cook until chicken is no longer pink and light brown on both sides.

3. Return chicken tenders that have been set aside to skillet. Stir in orange juice, soy sauce and ginger. Cover and simmer for about 10 minutes. Add mandarin orange sections and simmer for an additional 5 minutes.

Nutrition Facts
Serving Size 1 cup (250 ml)
Servings Per Recipe 4
Amount Per Serving
Calories 211
Total Fat 0g
Cholesterol 99mg
Sodium 362mg
Total Carbohydrate 14g
Dietary Fiber 0g
Sugars 7g
Protein 35g

Chicken Waldorf Salad

2 red delicious apples with peels, cored, diced	
1 tablespoon fresh lemon juice	15 ml
1½ cups seedless red or green grapes, halved	225 g
1 cup diced celery	100 g
3 cups cooked, cubed chicken breast	420 g
½ cup reduced-fat mayonnaise	110 g

1. Sprinkle apples with lemon juice to prevent browning.

2. Combine apples, grapes, celery, chicken and mayonnaise in large bowl.

Nutrition Facts

Serving Size 1 cup (250 ml)
Servings Per Recipe 8

Amount Per Serving	
Calories 149	
Total Fat 7g	
Cholesterol 46mg	
Sodium 163mg	
Total Carbohydrate 7g	
Dietary Fiber 0g	
Sugars 5g	
Protein 16g	

Turkey Pita Lunch

2 whole wheat pita breads	
2 tablespoons dijon-style mustard	30 g
8 thin slices deli turkey	
2 cups fresh vegetables (alfalfa spouts, cucumber and tomato slices)	285 g
2 tablespoons sunflower seeds	15 g

1. Cut pita breads in half and spread with mustard. Fill each half with 2 slices turkey and one-fourth fresh vegetables. Garnish with one-fourth sunflower seeds.

Nutrition Facts

Serving Size ½ pita bread
Servings Per Recipe 4

Amount Per Serving	
Calories 149	
Total Fat 4g	
Cholesterol 13mg	
Sodium 430mg	
Total Carbohydrate 23g	
Dietary Fiber 3g	
Sugars 3g	
Protein 9g	

Crunchy Turkey Slaw

Great way to use leftover turkey!

1 cup cooked, diced turkey	140 g
5 cups finely shredded green cabbage	350 g
1 cup sliced celery	100 g
3 tablespoons Soy Sauce Dressing (page 140)	45 ml
¼ cup toasted crushed ramen noodles	15 g

1. Lightly toss turkey, cabbage and celery in large bowl.

2. Drizzle with Soy Sauce Dressing and toss lightly. Sprinkle with ramen noodles.

Nutrition Facts
Serving Size 1 cup (250 ml)
Servings Per Recipe 6
Amount Per Serving
Calories 82
Total Fat 3g
Cholesterol 18mg
Sodium 133mg
Total Carbohydrate 3g
Dietary Fiber 2g
Sugars 3g
Protein 8g

Juicy Turkey Burgers

½ cup finely chopped onions	80 g
2 slices low-carb wheat bread	
1 (1 pound) package ground turkey breast	455 g
1 cup grated zucchini	125 g
2 tablespoons reduced-fat mayonnaise	30 g

1. Cook and stir onions in sprayed skillet over medium heat until tender, adding few drops water if needed. Remove from skillet and set aside.

2. Pulse bread in food processor or blender until crumbs are fine. (Breadcrumbs should measure 1 cup/60 g).

3. Lightly mix onion, breadcrumbs, turkey, zucchini and mayonnaise in bowl.

4. Form mixture into 5 patties. Place patties in sprayed skillet over medium heat and cook for 3 to 4 minutes on each side. Do not overcook.

Nutrition Facts
Serving Size 1 patty
Servings Per Recipe 5
Amount Per Serving
Calories 87
Total Fat 3g
Cholesterol 20mg
Sodium 118mg
Total Carbohydrate 7g
Dietary Fiber 1g
Sugars 2g
Protein 9g

Chunky Sloppy Joes

½ pound ground white turkey breast	230 g
1 cup frozen pepper stir-fry (sliced green, red, yellow bell peppers and white onions)	140 g
¼ cup no-salt tomato sauce	60 g
¼ cup fat-free barbecue sauce	70 g
4 sugar-free whole wheat hamburger buns	

1. Brown turkey in sprayed non-stick skillet over medium heat. Remove from skillet and set aside.

2. In same skillet, cook and stir peppers and onions until they brown lightly.

3. Return cooked turkey to skillet and add tomato sauce, barbecue sauce and 3 to 4 tablespoons (45 to 60 ml) water. Simmer for about 8 minutes and add water if needed. Serve on hamburger buns.

Nutrition Facts
Serving Size ½ cup (125 ml)
Servings Per Recipe 4
Amount Per Serving
Calories 167
Total Fat 2g
Cholesterol 11mg
Sodium 449mg
Total Carbohydrate 30g
Dietary Fiber 2g
Sugars 5g
Protein 11g

Spaghetti and Meatballs

1 (12 ounce) package reduced-carb spaghetti	340 g
1 (12 ounce) package frozen Italian-style turkey meatballs	340 g
1 (8 ounce) package fresh mushrooms, sliced	230 g
3 cups Homemade Marinara Sauce (page 233)	750 ml

1. Prepare spaghetti according to package directions.

2. Heat meatballs according to package directions.

3. Cook and stir mushrooms in sprayed skillet over medium heat for 5 minutes or until tender.

4. Combine mushrooms, meatballs and marinara sauce. Serve 1 meatball and ¼ cup (60 ml) sauce with ½ cup (95 g) cooked spaghetti.

Nutrition Facts

Serving Size 1 meatball with pasta and sauce
Servings Per Recipe 12

Amount Per Serving
Calories 194
Total Fat 4g
Cholesterol 23mg
Sodium 503mg
Total Carbohydrate 23g
Dietary Fiber 3g
Sugars 4g
Protein 10g

Low-Cal Low-Carb Lasagna

5 zucchini, cut in lengthwise slices	
1 pound ground turkey breast	455 g
2 cups Easy Pasta Sauce (page 235)	500 ml
1 cup shredded reduced-fat mozzarella cheese	115 g

1. Preheat oven to 350° (175° C).

2. Heat ½ cup (125 ml) water in 12-inch (32 cm) skillet until it boils. Add zucchini, reduce heat, cover and simmer until zucchini is clear and tender. Drain and set aside.

3. Spray in same skillet and cook and stir turkey until turkey turns white.

4. Add pasta sauce and ¼ cup (60 ml) water. Simmer for 15 to 20 minutes to blend flavors.

5. Place zucchini in sprayed 9 x 13-inch (23 x 33 cm) baking dish in single layer. Pour meat sauce over zucchini. Cover and bake for 15 to 20 minutes or until mixture bubbles and heats through.

6. Uncover and sprinkle with cheese. Return to oven for 5 minutes or until cheese melts.

Nutrition Facts
Serving Size 1 cup (250 ml)
Servings Per Recipe 10
Amount Per Serving
Calories 117
Total Fat 4g
Cholesterol 23mg
Sodium 315mg
Total Carbohydrate 6g
Dietary Fiber 2g
Sugars 3g
Protein 15g

Mexican Meat Loaf

1 (14 ounce) can stewed tomatoes with Mexican flavors (jalapeno, garlic and cumin), divided	400 g
1 (1 pound) package ground turkey breast	455 g
½ cup liquid egg substitute	120 g
1 cup old-fashioned oats	80 g

1. Preheat oven to 350° (175° C).

2. Process tomatoes in food processor or blender for about 5 to 10 seconds. Combine all ingredients in large bowl.

3. Pack mixture in sprayed 9 x 5-inch (23 x 13 cm) loaf pan.

4. Bake for 1 hour 30 minutes. Drain fat from loaf pan 1 to 2 times during cooking.

Nutrition Facts
Serving Size 1 (1 inch/2.5 cm) slice
Servings Per Recipe 6
Amount Per Serving
Calories 215
Total Fat 12g
Cholesterol 51mg
Sodium 410mg
Total Carbohydrate 9g
Dietary Fiber less than 1g
Sugars 4g
Protein 17g

Spaghetti Meat Sauce

1 pound ground turkey breast	455 g
3 cups Homemade Marinara Sauce	
(page 233)	750 ml
1 - 2 teaspoons Italian herb blend	5 - 10 ml

1. Cook turkey in sprayed large skillet over medium heat until it browns. Drain in strainer. Wipe skillet with paper towels to remove any excess fat.

2. Return turkey to skillet and add Homemade Marinara Sauce, herbs and 1 cup (250 ml) water and mix well. Cover and simmer for 30 minutes to allow flavors to blend.

Nutrition Facts

Serving Size ½ cup (125 ml)
Servings Per Recipe 8

Amount Per Serving	
Calories 166	
Total Fat 10g	
Cholesterol 42mg	
Sodium 437mg	
Total Carbohydrate 5g	
Dietary Fiber 1g	
Sugars 3g	
Protein 12g	

Pepperoni Pita-Pizza

2 (6 inch) whole wheat pita breads, split	2 (15 cm)
¾ cup Homemade Marinara Sauce (page 233)	175 ml
24 slices turkey pepperoni	
½ cup finely shredded part-skim	
mozzarella cheese	60 g

1. Lightly toast split pita bread. Spread each with one-fourth Homemade Marinara Sauce. Add 6 slices pepperoni and one-fourth cheese on each pita half.

2. Broil for 2 to 3 minutes or until cheese melts.

Nutrition Facts

Serving Size 1 pita half
Servings Per Recipe 4

Amount Per Serving	
Calories 173	
Total Fat 4g	
Cholesterol 2mg	
Sodium 503mg	
Total Carbohydrate 23g	
Dietary Fiber 3g	
Sugars 4g	
Protein 10g	

Turkey Soft Tacos

1 pound ground turkey breast	455 g
6 teaspoons Reduced-Sodium Taco Seasoning (page 238)	30 ml
6 (8 inch) low-carb whole wheat tortillas	6 (20 cm)
½ cup finely shredded reduced-fat cheddar cheese	57 g
1½ cups shredded iceberg lettuce	116 g
½ cup chopped fresh tomatoes	90 g
Salsa	

1. Brown turkey in sprayed 10-inch (25 cm) skillet over medium heat. Stir in ⅔ cup (150 ml) water and Reduced-Sodium Taco Seasoning to skillet. Bring to a boil and reduce heat to simmer. Cook and stir for 3 to 4 minutes until flavors blend and sauce thickens.

2. Spoon one-sixth turkey onto each tortilla. Sprinkle each with one-sixth cheese, lettuce and tomato. Fold over or roll. Garnish with salsa.

Nutrition Facts
Serving Size 1 taco
Servings Per Recipe 6
Amount Per Serving
Calories 220
Total Fat 7g
Cholesterol 60mg
Sodium 402mg
Total Carbohydrate 12g
Dietary Fiber 8g
Sugars 0g
Protein 26

Turkey Sausage, Cabbage and Carrots

1 onion, sliced	
1 garlic clove, minced	
2 carrots, sliced diagonally	
2 cups shredded green cabbage	140 g
1 cup 98% fat-free chicken broth	250 ml
1 pound precooked turkey sausage, sliced	
diagonally	455 g

1. Cook and stir onion, garlic and carrots in large sprayed heavy pan over medium heat until tender. Add cabbage and cook and stir for 3 to 4 minutes. Pour in chicken broth and bring to a boil. Reduce heat and simmer until cabbage is tender.

2. Add turkey sausage and heat through.

Nutrition Facts
Serving Size 1 cup (250 ml)
Servings Per Recipe 6
Amount Per Serving
Calories 142
Total Fat 7g
Cholesterol 40mg
Sodium 872mg
Total Carbohydrate 9g
Dietary Fiber 2g
Sugars 5g
Protein 12g

Cornish Hens with Cran-Orange Relish

2 (1¼ - 1½ pound) frozen cornish hens	2 (570 - 680 g)
2 oranges	
¼ cup Craisins®	30 g
1 tablespoon chopped pecans	15 ml

1. Thaw hens and roast according to package directions.

2. While hens roast, prepare orange relish. Grate 2 teaspoons (10 ml) orange peel, remove peel, separate into sections and cut in ½-inch (1.2 cm) pieces.

3. Combine orange pieces, Craisins® and pecans in small bowl. Transfer to serving dish and sprinkle orange peel on top. Cover and refrigerate until serving time.

4. When ready to serve, cut hens in half lengthwise. Serve with fresh orange relish.

Nutrition Facts
Serving Size ½ hen and ¼ cup (60 ml) relish
Servings Per Recipe 4
Amount Per Serving
Calories 407
Total Fat 3g
Cholesterol 168mg
Sodium 84mg
Total Carbohydrate 16g
Dietary Fiber 2g
Sugars 11g
Protein 30g

Hot Dog Wraps

4 (8 inch) low-carb whole wheat tortillas   4 (20 cm)
4 regular size fat-free frankfurters
4 mozzarella string cheese sticks, pulled apart
Condiments (pickle relish, mustard, sugar-free ketchup)

1. Preheat oven to 375° (190° C).

2. Spray one side of tortillas with cooking spray and place frankfurter about 1 inch (2.5 cm) from edge of each tortilla.

3. Split frankfurter down middle and insert string cheese. Add condiments. Roll frankfurter inside tortilla.

4. Arrange tortillas seam-side down on sprayed baking sheet. Spray tops of tortillas.

5. Bake for 10 to 15 minutes or until cheese melts.

Nutrition Facts
Serving size 1 hot dog wrap
Servings Per Recipe 4
Amount Per Serving
Calories 231
Total Fat 7g
Cholesterol 62mg
Sodium 993mg
Total Carbohydrate 25g
Dietary Fiber 11g
Sugars 2g
Protein 18g

Pork Medallions with Apples and Onions

1 (¾ to 1 pound) pork tenderloin   340 - 455 g
1 onion
1 Granny Smith apple
½ cup 98% fat-free chicken broth, divided   125 ml

1. Cut tenderloin in ¾-inch (1.8 cm) crosswise slices.

2. Peel onion, cut in half and cut each half into slices. Plea and core apple and cut into thin slices.

3. Brown medallions in sprayed 10-inch (25 cm) skillet over medium-high heat. Remove and set aside. Add sliced onions and apples. Stir and cook until light brown.

4. Return pork medallions to skillet. Add ⅓ cup (75 ml) chicken broth and bring to a boil. Reduce heat to simmer. Cook for about 5 minutes and add remaining chicken broth if needed. Remove pork, onions and apples and keep warm in serving dish.

5. Cook sauce from skillet over medium-high until it thickens slightly. Spoon sauce over pork.

TIP: *A medallion is a small, round piece of meat, usually beef, veal or pork.*

Nutrition Facts
Serving size 1 pork medallion
Servings Per Recipe 6
Amount Per Serving
Calories 139
Total Fat 5g
Cholesterol 52mg
Sodium 71mg
Total Carbohydrate 4g
Dietary Fiber less than 1g
Sugars 3g
Protein 18g

Ham-Cheese-Asparagus Rolls

½ pound fresh medium asparagus spears,
    trimmed   230 g
8 slices 96% fat-free deli ham
2 part-skim mozzarella string cheese sticks,
    pulled apart
½ cup Spicy Mustard Sauce (page 237)   125 ml

1. Preheat oven to 325° (160° C).

2. Cook asparagus spears in small amount of boiling water in 10-inch (25 cm) skillet until tender-crisp. Do not overcook. Drain.

3. For each roll, assemble 2 slices ham, 3 asparagus spears and one-half cheese stick. Roll ham lengthwise around asparagus and cheese and secure with toothpicks. Place ham rolls in sprayed 9-inch (23 cm) square baking dish. Cover and bake for 15 minutes or until cheese melts.

4. Spoon warmed Spicy Mustard Sauce over each serving.

Nutrition Facts	
Serving size 1 ham roll	
Servings Per Recipe 4	
Amount Per Serving	
Calories 102	
Total Fat 3g	
Cholesterol 10mg	
Sodium 262mg	
Total Carbohydrate 9g	
Dietary Fiber 1g	
Sugars 5g	
Protein 10g	

Broiled Pork Chops with Apples

4 (3 x 4 inch) boneless pork chops   4 (8 x 10 cm)
1 cup Maple Stir-Fry Apples (page 243)   250 ml

1. Preheat oven broiler.

2. Place pork chops in broiler pan. Broil for 10 minutes on each side. Serve with Maple Stir-Fry Apples.

Nutrition Facts
Serving size 1 pork chop with apples
Servings Per Recipe 4
Amount Per Serving
Calories 206
Total Fat 7g
Cholesterol 62mg
Sodium 43mg
Total Carbohydrate 10g
Dietary Fiber 2g
Sugars 7g
Protein 25g

Shrimp-Avocado Salad

1 head romaine or leaf lettuce
1 ripe avocado
½ pound cooked, peeled, veined shrimp   230 g
Lemon wedges

1. Cut out large lettuce ribs or stems with knife. Roll lettuce and hold while cutting in ¼-inch (6 mm) pieces. Pile lettuce on 4 salad plates.

2. Halve avocado and remove seed. With peel still on, cut half into 4 wedges. Carefully pull peel away with fingers. Arrange wedges on lettuce.

3. Arrange shrimp on top of avocado. Serve with lemon wedges.

Nutrition Facts
Serving size 1½ cups (375 ml)
Servings Per Recipe 4
Amount Per Serving
Calories 163
Total Fat 8g
Cholesterol 110mg
Sodium 143mg
Total Carbohydrate 9g
Dietary Fiber 7g
Sugars 2g
Protein 15g

Rebecca's Shrimp Florentine

2 (10 ounce) bags fresh spinach   2 (280 g)
1 tablespoon cornstarch   15 ml
2 pounds frozen cooked, peeled,
    veined shrimp   910 g
Lemon-pepper seasoning

1. Cook spinach in large sprayed skillet over medium
    heat for 3 to 5 minutes or until it is limp.

2. Mix cornstarch with 1 tablespoon
    (15 ml) water in bowl and stir
    until it dissolves. Add cornstarch
    mixture to skillet, bring to boil
    and stir until it thickens.

3. Add shrimp and a little lemon-
    pepper seasoning. Reduce heat
    to low and cook until shrimp
    heats through.

Nutrition Facts
Serving size 1 cup (250 ml) Servings Per Recipe 8
Amount Per Serving
Calories 140
Total Fat 2g
Cholesterol 172mg
Sodium 313mg
Total Carbohydrate 4g
Dietary Fiber 1g
Sugars 0g
Protein 25g

Speedy Shrimp Creole

1 (12 ounce) package frozen seasoning blend (onions, celery, peppers, parsley), thawed	340 g
1 cup sliced fresh mushrooms	70 g
1 (14 ounce) can diced tomatoes with liquid	400 g
1 pound fresh, peeled, veined shrimp	455 g
Hot pepper sauce	

1. Cook and stir seasoning blend and mushrooms in 10-inch (25 cm) skillet over medium heat until vegetables are tender and liquid evaporates. Add tomatoes and simmer for 15 to 20 minutes.

2. Add shrimp and a little hot pepper sauce and cook until shrimp turn pink and are tender.

Nutrition Facts

Serving size 1 cup (250 ml)
Servings Per Recipe 4

Amount Per Serving
Calories 166
Total Fat 1g
Cholesterol 221mg
Sodium 327mg
Total Carbohydrate 11g
Dietary Fiber 3g
Sugars 7g
Protein 25g

Spicy Crawfish Sauce

1 (10 ounce) can diced tomatoes and green chilies	280 g
1 (16 ounce) package frozen cleaned, peeled crawfish tails	455 g
1 (10 ounce) can reduced-fat cream of chicken soup	280 g
8 ounces Velveeta® cheese, 2% milk	225 g

1. Add tomatoes and green chilies to 10-inch (25 cm) skillet and cook for 3 minutes or until hot.

2. Add crawfish and cook and stir for 10 minutes.

3. Add soup and cheese; cook until mixture heats through.

Nutrition Facts

Serving size ½ cup (125 ml)
Servings Per Recipe 11

Amount per Serving

Calories 100

Total Fat 3g

Cholesterol 53mg

Sodium 565mg

Total Carbohydrate 7g

Dietary Fiber 0

Sugars 2g

Protein 11g

Low-Fat Salmon Patties

1 (12 ounce) can salmon	340 g
⅓ cup finely chopped onion	55 g
¼ cup liquid egg substitute	60 g
11 multigrain or reduced-fat saltine crackers, crushed, divided	

1. Drain salmon and remove excess skin. Flake with fork in bowl. Stir in onion, egg substitute and ¼ cup (15 g) cracker crumbs.

2. Pack salmon mixture for each patty into ⅓ cup (75 ml). Remove, flatten slightly and coat with crushed crackers.

3. Preheat non-stick skillet over high heat. Liberally spray 1 side of each patty with cooking spray. Place patty sprayed-side down in skillet. Reduce heat to medium.

4. Cook each patty in sprayed 10-inch (25 cm) skillet over medium-high heat for 3 minutes. Spray top of patty and turn carefully with spatula. Cook for 2 to 3 more minutes or until patty turns golden brown.

Nutrition Facts
Serving size 1 patty
Servings Per Recipe 6
Amount Per Serving
Calories 129
Total Fat 4g
Cholesterol 20mg
Sodium 434mg
Total Carbohydrate 9g
Dietary Fiber less than 1g
Sugars 2g
Protein 12g

Heart Healthy Tuna Melts

1 (7 ounce) package solid white albacore tuna in water, drained	200 g
2 tablespoons reduced-fat mayonnaise	30 g
8 slices low-carb wheat bread	
4 slices fat-free sharp cheddar cheese	

1. Break tuna into small flakes with fork in small bowl. Add mayonnaise and mix well.

2. Spread tuna mixture evenly on 4 slices bread and top with cheese and bread slice.

3. Place 1 sandwich in 10-inch (25 cm) sprayed skillet on medium-high heat and cook on one side until it browns. Spray top of sandwich, turn over and cook until it browns.

4. Repeat with remaining 3 sandwiches.

Nutrition Facts
Serving size 1 sandwich
Servings Per Recipe 4
Amount Per Serving
Calories 195
Total Fat 4g
Cholesterol 23mg
Sodium 873mg
Total Carbohydrate 17g
Dietary Fiber 4g
Sugars 3g
Protein 30g

Bill's Broiled Catfish Fillets

This is a no-brainer recipe and so-o-o-o delicious!

4 (4 ounce) catfish fillets   4 (115 g)
2 teaspoons Creole or Cajun seasoning, divided   10 ml
Lemon wedges

1. Preheat broiler.

2. Pat fillets dry with paper towels. Transfer fillets to wax paper or foil. Spray and lightly season fillets on both sides.

3. Arrange fillets in broiler pan and broil each side for about 6 minutes or until fish has crisped and flakes easily with fork.

4. Serve with lemon wedges.

TIP: Other fish, such as tilapia, work equally well in this recipe.

Nutrition Facts	
Serving size 1 fillet	
Servings Per Recipe 4	
Amount Per Serving	
Calories 152	
Total Fat 9g	
Cholesterol 53mg	
Sodium 406mg	
Total Carbohydrate 0g	
Dietary Fiber 0g	
Sugars 0g	
Protein 18g	

Grilled Portobello Burgers

½ cup Balsamic Vinaigrette (page 133)
4 large portobello mushroom caps
    (about 1 pound)   455 g
4 sugar-free wheat hamburger buns
Burger "fixin's" (lettuce, tomato slices, onion rings)

1. Preheat gas grill to medium heat or prepare charcoal grill.

2. Pour vinaigrette into shaker bottle.

3. Sprinkle mushroom caps with one-half Balsamic Vinaigrette and grill for about 6 minutes. Turn, sprinkle with remaining vinaigrette and grill for about 6 minutes or until softened.

4. Toast hamburger buns while mushroom caps are grilling. When mushroom caps are done, place onto toasted bun and add "fixin's." If you wish, drizzle with more vinaigrette.

Nutrition Facts	
Serving size 1 burger	
Servings Per Recipe 4	
Amount Per Serving	
Calories 193	
Total Fat 7g	
Cholesterol 0mg	
Sodium 191mg	
Total Carbohydrate 24g	
Dietary Fiber 5g	
Sugars 4g	
Protein 8g	

Black Bean Quesadillas

1 cup canned black beans, drained, rinsed	170 g
1 cup mild or medium salsa, divided	265 g
12 (8 inch) low carb whole wheat tortillas	12 (20 cm)
1 cup shredded reduced-fat colby Jack cheese	115 g
¼ cup chopped green onions with tops	25 g
1 tablespoon chopped fresh cilantro	15 ml

1. Mash beans with fork in bowl and combine with ¼ cup (65 g) salsa.

2. Spray tortillas on both sides with non-stick cooking spray. Spoon bean mixture evenly on 6 tortillas, spreading almost to edges. Sprinkle evenly with cheese, green onions and cilantro. Top with remaining tortillas.

3. Preheat sprayed griddle or skillet over medium heat until hot. Place 1 quesadilla on griddle and cook for 2 to 3 minutes or until it begins to brown. Turn and cook for 1 to 2 minutes.

4. Repeat with remaining quesadillas. Cut each into 6 wedges and serve hot with remaining salsa.

Nutrition Facts

Serving Size 3 wedges
Servings Per Recipe 12

Amount Per Serving
Calories 133
Total Fat 7g
Cholesterol 14mg
Sodium 361mg
Total Carbohydrate 15g
Dietary Fiber 9g
Sugars less than 1g
Protein 11g

Veggie Tacos

1 cup veggie protein crumbles	110 g
¼ cup salsa	65 g
4 (6 inch) taco shells	4 (15 cm)
¼ cup finely shredded reduced-fat colby Jack cheese	30 g

1. Preheat oven to 350° (175° C).

2. Combine veggie crumbles, salsa and 3 tablespoons (45 ml) water in 10-inch (25 cm) skillet over low heat.

3. Heat taco shells on baking sheet for 5 to 6 minutes or until hot and crisp.

4. Spoon one-fourth mixture into each taco shell and sprinkle with one-fourth cheese.

TIP: *Serve with shredded iceberg lettuce and chopped tomatoes.*

Nutrition Facts
Serving Size 1 taco
Servings Per Recipe 4
Amount Per Serving
Calories 135
Total Fat 7g
Cholesterol 10mg
Sodium 283mg
Total Carbohydrate 11g
Dietary Fiber 2g
Sugars less than 1g
Protein 8g

All-Purpose Green Chili Sauce

1 tablespoon butter	15 ml
½ cup finely chopped onion	80 g
1 garlic clove, minced	
1½ tablespoons flour	22 ml
1½ cups 98% fat-free chicken broth	375 ml
1 (4 ounce) can chopped green chilies with liquid	115 g
Ground cumin	

1. Melt butter in heavy saucepan over medium heat. Add onion and garlic and cook until tender. Stir in flour, cook and stir until mixture bubbles. Cook for 1 minute.

2. Gradually stir in broth and bring to a boil. Cook and stir for 1 minute. Add green chilies and a little cumin; simmer for 15 to 20 minutes.

Nutrition Facts
Serving Size ¼ cup (60 ml)
Servings Per Recipe 6
Amount Per Serving
Calories 31
Total Fat 2g
Cholesterol 0mg
Sodium 219mg
Total Carbohydrate 3g
Dietary Fiber less than 1g
Sugars less than 1g
Protein 1g

Red Chili Enchilada Sauce

1 onion, finely chopped
2 cloves garlic, finely minced or pressed
3½ cups no salt tomato sauce   855 g
2 - 4 tablespoons chili powder, divided   15 - 30 g
¼ teaspoon ground cumin   1 ml
¼ teaspoon dried oregano, crushed   1 ml

1. Cook and stir onion and garlic in 2-quart (2 L) saucepan over medium heat until onion is clear and tender.

2. Add tomato sauce and bring to a boil. Gradually stir in 2 tablespoons (15 g) chili powder, cumin and oregano.

3. Reduce heat and simmer for 30 minutes. Add remaining chili powder if you want it spicier.

Nutrition Facts
Serving Size ¼ cup (60 ml)
Servings Per Recipe 12
Amount Per Serving
Calories 31
Total Fat less than 1g
Cholesterol 0mg
Sodium 35mg
Total Carbohydrate 0g
Dietary Fiber 2g
Sugars 5g
Protein 2g

Reduced-Fat Pesto Spread

Emergency pantry pesto spread.

2 tablespoon pine nuts	15 g
4 teaspoons crushed basil leaves	20 ml
½ teaspoon finely minced garlic	2 ml
½ teaspoon olive oil	2 ml

1. Stir and toast pine nuts in dry skillet over low heat until they brown lightly. Do not burn.

2. Crush pine nuts, using wooden cutting board and rolling pin (or mortar and pestle).

3. Combine crushed pine nuts, basil, garlic and olive oil in bowl until they mix well.

Nutrition Facts
Serving Size 1 teaspoon (5 ml)
Servings Per Recipe 10
Amount Per Serving
Calories 14
Total Fat 1g
Cholesterol 0mg
Sodium 0mg
Total Carbohydrate 0g
Dietary Fiber 0g
Sugars 0g
Protein 0g

Homemade Marinara Sauce

1 (12 ounce) package frozen seasoning blend
    (onions, celery, peppers, parsley), thawed   340 g
2 cloves garlic, finely minced
3 cups no salt tomato sauce   730 g
2 teaspoons Italian herb seasoning blend   10 ml

1. Cook and stir seasoning blend and garlic in 2-quart (2 L) saucepan over medium heat until vegetables are tender.

2. Add tomato sauce and herb blend and bring to a boil.

3. Reduce heat, cover and simmer for 10 to 15 minutes for flavors to blend.

Nutrition Facts	
Serving Size ¼ cup (60 ml)	
Servings Per Recipe 12	
Amount Per Serving	
Calories 30	
Total Fat 0g	
Cholesterol 0mg	
Sodium 29mg	
Total Carbohydrate 6g	
Dietary Fiber less than 1g	
Sugars 5g	
Protein less than 1g	

Sweet-and-Sour Sauce

Granular sugar substitute to equal ½ cup
      (100 g) sugar
1 tablespoon cornstarch   15 ml
⅓ cup rice or white wine vinegar   75 ml
1 tablespoon reduced-sodium soy sauce   15 ml

1. Combine sugar substitute and cornstarch in medium saucepan.

2. Stir in ½ cup (125 ml) water, vinegar and soy sauce and mix well.

3. Heat mixture over medium heat until it boils, stirring constantly. Boil and stir for 1 minute.

Nutrition Facts
Serving Size 1 tablespoon (15 ml)
Servings Per Recipe 12
Amount Per Serving
Calories 8
Total Fat 0g
Cholesterol 0mg
Sodium 58mg
Total Carbohydrate 2g
Dietary Fiber 0g
Sugars less than 1g
Protein less than 1g

Easy Pasta Sauce

1 clove garlic, finely minced	
2 (8 ounce) cans no salt tomato sauce	2 (230 g)
1 teaspoon dried basil, crushed	5 ml
½ teaspoon dried oregano, crushed	2 ml

1. Cook and stir garlic in sprayed 1-quart (1 L) saucepan over medium heat for about 1 minute. Do not burn.

2. Add tomato sauce, basil and oregano. Heat mixture until it boils, then reduce heat and simmer for 5 to 6 minutes.

Nutrition Facts	
Serving Size ½ cup (125 ml) Servings Per Recipe 4	
Amount Per Serving	
Calories 39	
Total Fat less than 1g	
Cholesterol 0mg	
Sodium 37mg	
Total Carbohydrate 8g	
Dietary Fiber 1g	
Sugars 7g	
Protein 1g	

Low-Carb Barbecue Sauce

½ cup ketchup	135 g
⅓ cup cider vinegar	75 ml
1 tablespoon molasses	15 ml
1 teaspoon dry barbecue seasoning mix	5 ml

1. Whisk all ingredients in small bowl. Store in refrigerator.

TIP: *This recipe makes a great sauce, even without the seasoning mix.*

Nutrition Facts	
Serving Size 1 tablespoon (15 ml) Servings Per Recipe 12	
Amount Per Serving	
Calories 17	
Total Fat 0g	
Cholesterol 0mg	
Sodium 129mg	
Total Carbohydrate 4g	
Dietary Fiber 0g	
Sugars 3g	
Protein 0g	

Make Your Own Cheese Sauce

2 tablespoons butter	30 g
2 tablespoons all-purpose flour	15 g
1¼ cups fat-free milk	310 ml
¼ cup shredded reduced-fat cheddar cheese	30 g

1. Melt butter in heavy saucepan over medium heat. Add flour, cook and stir for about 2 minutes. Do not brown.

2. Add milk and heat until it boils, stirring constantly. Reduce heat and cook for 2 to 3 minutes until sauce thickens.

3. Add cheese and stir until cheese melts.

Nutrition Facts

Serving Size ¼ cup (60 ml)
Servings Per Recipe 4

Amount Per Serving
Calories 111
Total Fat 7g
Cholesterol 22mg
Sodium 180mg
Total Carbohydrate 7g
Dietary Fiber less than 1g
Sugars 4g
Protein 7g

Spicy Mustard Sauce

2 tablespoons butter	30 g
2 tablespoons all-purpose flour	15 g
2 cups fat-free milk	500 ml
2 tablespoons dijon-style mustard	30 g

1. Melt butter in 2-quart (2 L) saucepan over medium heat. Stir in flour and mix well.

2. Add milk, stirring constantly until mixture boils. Boil for 1 minute until mixture thickens and becomes smooth.

3. Remove from heat and stir in mustard.

Nutrition Facts

Serving Size 2 tablespoons (30 ml)
Servings Per Recipe 16

Amount Per Serving

Calories 27

Total Fat 1g

Cholesterol less than 1mg

Sodium 92mg

Total Carbohydrate 3g

Dietary Fiber less than 1g

Sugars 2g

Protein 2g

Stir-Fry Cooking Sauce

4 teaspoons cornstarch	20 ml
2 teaspoons reduced-sodium soy sauce	10 ml
½ teaspoon ground ginger	1 ml
2 tablespoons cooking sherry or water	30 ml

1. Combine all ingredients in small bowl and stir until cornstarch dissolves. Stir again before using.

Nutrition Facts

Serving Size 1 tablespoon (15 ml)
Servings Per Recipe 4

Amount Per Serving

Calories 18

Total Fat 0g

Cholesterol 0mg

Sodium 120mg

Total Carbohydrate 3g

Dietary Fiber less than 1g

Sugars less than 1g

Protein less than 1g

Reduced-Sodium Taco Seasoning

Seasoning for 1 pound (455 g) ground beef.

Salt substitute to equal 1½ teaspoons (7 ml) salt
1 teaspoon ground cumin	5 ml
2¼ teaspoons chili powder	11 ml
1 teaspoon garlic powder	5 ml
½ teaspoon onion powder	2 ml
¼ teaspoon red pepper	1 ml
1 teaspoon cornstarch	5 ml

1. Combine ingredients in bowl. Use or store in freezer.

Nutrition Facts

Serving Size 1 teaspoon (5 ml) dry mix
Servings Per Recipe 6

Amount Per Serving
Calories 1
Total Fat 0g
Cholesterol 0mg
Sodium 14mg
Total Carbohydrate 0g
Dietary Fiber 0g
Sugars 0g
Protein 0g

Desserts

Desserts Contents

Kiwi Delight

3 large kiwifruit
Sugar substitute to equal 2 tablespoons
    (25 g) sugar
1 cup reduced-fat whipped topping, thawed   75 g
⅛ teaspoon vanilla   .5 ml

1. Peel kiwifruit. Cut 1 kiwifruit crosswise in half and
    set aside 1 half for garnish. Cut remaining kiwifruit
    into chunks.

2. Blend kiwifruit and sugar substitute in blender or
    food processor on medium speed
    until smooth.

3. Lightly mix blended kiwifruit,
    whipped topping and vanilla
    in bowl.

4. Spoon kiwifruit mixture into
    4 parfait or stemmed glass
    and garnish with reserved
    kiwifruit slices.

Nutrition Facts
Serving Size ½ cup (125 ml)
Servings Per Recipe 4
Amount Per Serving
Calories 80
Total Fat 2g
Cholesterol 0mg
Sodium 1mg
Total Carbohydrate 13g
Dietary Fiber 2g
Sugars 8g
Protein less than 1g

Apple-Pecan Crunch

1 (20 ounce) can reduced-sugar apple pie filling   570 g
20 sugar-free vanilla wafers
½ teaspoon ground cinnamon   2 ml
¼ cup chopped pecans   30 g

1. Preheat oven to 300° (150° C).

2. Chop apple pie filling into small pieces.

3. Coarsely crush vanilla wafers in bowl. Stir cinnamon and pecans into crushed wafers.

4. Spray 6 ovenproof custard cups. Spoon 2 tablespoons (35 g) pie filling and 1 tablespoon (15 ml) wafer mixture into each cup. Repeat layers.

5. Bake for 20 minutes or until pie filling bubbles and heats through.

Nutrition Facts
Serving Size 1 custard cup
Servings Per Recipe 6
Amount Per Serving
Calories 108
Total Fat 5g
Cholesterol 0mg
Sodium 35mg
Total Carbohydrate 16g
Dietary Fiber less than 1g
Sugars 6g
Protein 1g

Maple Stir-Fry Apples

2 Granny Smith apples with peels, cored,
     thinly sliced
1 - 2 tablespoons sugar-free maple syrup   15 - 30 ml

1. Cook and stir apples in sprayed 10-inch (25 cm) skillet
   over medium heat until brown on
   both sides.

2. Add ¼ cup (60 ml) water, cover
   and simmer for 10 to 15 minutes
   or until apples become tender.
   Remove cover, increase heat and
   stir until water evaporates.

3. Serve apples warm with
   maple syrup.

Nutrition Facts
Serving Size ¼ cup (60 ml)
Servings Per Recipe 4
Amount Per Serving
Calories 37
Total Fat less than 1g
Cholesterol 0mg
Sodium 2mg
Total Carbohydrate 10g
Dietary Fiber 2g
Sugars 7g
Protein less than 1g

Lime-Ginger Melon

4 teaspoons fresh lime juice	20 ml
Sugar substitute to equal ¼ cup (50 g) sugar	
¼ teaspoon ground ginger	1 ml
4 cups cubed watermelon, honeydew or cantaloupe	615 g/710 g
1 tablespoon grated lime peel	15 ml

1. Combine ½ cup (125 ml) water, lime juice, sugar substitute and ginger in 1-quart (1 L) saucepan. Heat to boiling. Remove from heat and cool to room temperature.

2. Place one-fourth melon cubes in each of 4 dessert bowls. Drizzle with lime juice mixture.

3. Garnish with grated lime peel.

Nutrition Facts

Serving Size 1 cup (250 ml)
Servings Per Recipe 4

Amount Per Serving
Calories 47
Total Fat less than 1g
Cholesterol 0mg
Sodium 2mg
Total Carbohydrate 14g
Dietary Fiber less than 1g
Sugars 10g
Protein less than 1g

Granny Smith's Apples

6 Granny Smith apples
1 cinnamon stick, broken
Sugar substitute to equal 2 tablespoons (25 g) sugar

1. Peel and core apples. Cut in ½-inch (1.2 cm) thick slices.

2. Place apples in 10-inch (25 cm) skillet with cinnamon stick and sugar substitute. Add ⅔ cup (150 ml) water.

3. Cover and simmer, stirring frequently, over low heat for about 20 minutes or until apples are tender but not mushy. Remove cinnamon before serving.

Nutrition Facts		
Serving Size ½ cup (125 ml) Servings Per Recipe 4		
Amount Per Serving		
Calories 111		
Total Fat less than 1g		
Cholesterol 0mg		
Sodium 2mg		
Total Carbohydrate 30g		
Dietary Fiber 6g		
Sugars 22g		
Protein less than 1g		

Pistachio-Double Strawberry Dessert

2 (1 ounce) packages instant sugar-free
  pistachio pudding mix   2 (30 g)
4 cups fat-free milk   1 L
1 prepared strawberry sugar-free angel food
  cake, bite-size pieces
3 cups sliced fresh strawberries, slightly crushed 500 g

1. Combine pudding mix and milk in bowl and mix well.
   Refrigerate for 4 to 5 minutes.

2. Place one-third cake pieces, one-third pudding and one-third strawberries in trifle bowl or large glass bowl.

3. Repeat layers twice more, ending with strawberries on top. Refrigerate.

TIP: *Garnish each serving with reduced-fat whipped topping.*

Nutrition Facts	
Serving Size ¾ cup (175 ml)	
Servings Per Recipe 10	
Amount Per Serving	
Calories 113	
Total Fat less than 1g	
Cholesterol 2mg	
Sodium 463mg	
Total Carbohydrate 26g	
Dietary Fiber 1g	
Sugars 6g	
Protein 5g	

Guiltless Fruit Parfaits

2 cups reduced-fat vanilla yogurt	455 g
1 tablespoon sugar-free fruit drink powder	15 ml
2 cups fresh fruit (sliced bananas,	
strawberries, blueberries or other fruit)	330 g
¼ cup reduced-fat whipped topping, thawed	20 g

1. Combine yogurt and drink powder in bowl.

2. Spoon one-fourth yogurt mixture and one-fourth fruit into 4 parfait or stemmed glasses.

3. Top each dessert with 1 tablespoon (15 ml) whipped topping before serving.

Nutrition Facts

Serving Size 1¼ cup (310 ml)
using strawberries
Servings Per Recipe 4

Amount Per Serving

Calories 141

Total Fat less than 2g

Cholesterol 6mg

Sodium 85mg

Total Carbohydrate 24g

Dietary Fiber 2g

Sugars 22g

Protein 7g

Poached Pears with Raspberry Sauce

Sugar substitute to equal ½ cup (100 g) sugar
Cinnamon stick
2 whole ripe pears, peeled, halved, cored
2 tablespoons 100% seedless raspberry
    spreadable fruit   40 g

1. Heat and stir 2 cups (500 ml) water, sugar substitute and cinnamon stick in small saucepan until water boils. Using slotted spoon, add pears to boiling syrup. Reduce heat to simmer.

2. Simmer pears for 6 to 7 minutes or until they are tender. Transfer each pear to dessert plate with slotted spoon.

3. Combine 1 tablespoon (15 ml) water and fruit spread in custard cup. Microwave on HIGH for about 15 seconds.

4. Drizzle 2 teaspoons (10 ml) fruit spread on each pear half. Serve warm.

Nutrition Facts
Serving Size ½ pear
Servings Per Recipe 4
Amount Per Serving
Calories 68
Total Fat less than 1g
Cholesterol 0mg
Sodium less than 1mg
Total Carbohydrate 21g
Dietary Fiber 3g
Sugars 12g
Protein less than 1g

White Chocolate-Strawberry Trifle

2 (1 ounce) packages sugar-free instant white
    chocolate pudding mix   2 (30 g)
4 cups fat-free milk   1 L
4 cups sliced fresh strawberries   665 g
1 (8 ounce) carton strawberry whipped
    topping, thawed   230 g

1. Combine pudding mix and milk in bowl and mix well.

2. Spread one-half pudding and one-half sliced strawberries in 2-quart (2 L) glass bowl or trifle bowl. Repeat layers.

3. Spoon strawberry whipped topping on top.

Nutrition Facts

Serving Size ½ cup (125 ml)
Servings Per Recipe 10

Amount Per Serving

Calories 125

Total Fat 4g

Cholesterol 0mg

Sodium 291mg

Total Carbohydrate 17g

Dietary Fiber 1g

Sugars 9g

Protein 3g

Chilled Cappuccino Dessert

1 (1 ounce) package sugar-free instant vanilla pudding mix	30 g
½ cup strong brewed decaffeinated coffee, chilled	125 ml
1½ cups fat-free milk	375 ml
1 cup reduced-fat whipped topping, thawed	75 g

1. Combine pudding mix, coffee and milk in bowl and mix well.

2. Spoon one-fourth pudding and one-fourth whipped topping into each of 4 dessert dishes.

3. Refrigerate before serving.

Nutrition Facts
Serving Size ¾ cup (175 ml)
Servings Per Recipe 4
Amount Per Serving
Calories 81
Total Fat 3g
Cholesterol 2mg
Sodium 136mg
Total Carbohydrate 10g
Dietary Fiber 0g
Sugars 9g
Protein 4g

Pumpkin Flan

1 (3 ounce) package flan mix with caramel packet	85 g
1½ cups fat-free milk	375 ml
1 cup canned solid-pack pumpkin	245 g
⅛ teaspoon pumpkin pie spice	.5 ml

1. Pour equal amounts caramel sauce into 4 custard cups.

2. Prepare flan mix according to package directions using 1½ cups (375 ml) milk in saucepan. After mixture boils, remove saucepan from heat and stir in pumpkin and pumpkin pie spice.

3. Slowly pour equal amounts flan mixture into each custard cup. Refrigerate for 1 to 2 hours.

4. When ready to serve, use table knife to loosen custard. Invert each custard cup onto small dessert plate so caramel sauce covers custard.

Nutrition Facts

Serving Size ½ cup (125 ml)
Servings Per Recipe 4

Amount Per Serving

Calories 84

Total Fat less than 1g

Cholesterol 1mg

Sodium 90mg

Total Carbohydrate 19g

Dietary Fiber 1g

Sugars 4g

Protein 3g

Sugar-Free Egg Custard

A smooth as silk, satisfying custard dessert

1¾ cups fat-free milk	425 g
Sugar substitute to equal ½ cup (100 g) sugar	
1 teaspoon vanilla	5 ml
1 cup liquid egg substitute	245 g

1. Preheat oven to 350° (175° C).

2. Heat milk in saucepan over medium heat just to boiling. Remove from heat and whisk in sugar substitute and vanilla. Continue to whisk while gradually adding egg substitute. Pour into 4 sprayed custard cups.

3. Place custard cups in baking pan filled with 1 inch (2.5 cm) hot water. Bake for 35 minutes or until knife inserted in center comes out clean. Serve warm or cold.

TIP: Sprinkle custards with ground nutmeg before baking.

Nutrition Facts	
Serving Size ½ cup (125 ml) Servings Per Recipe 4	
Amount Per Serving	
Calories 69	
Total Fat 0g	
Cholesterol 2mg	
Sodium 162mg	
Total Carbohydrate 9g	
Dietary Fiber 0g	
Sugars 6g	
Protein 10g	

Speedy Banana Pudding

2 (1 ounce) packages sugar-free instant vanilla pudding mix	2 (30 g)
4 cups fat-free milk	1 L
3 bananas	
1 (6.5 ounce) package sugar-free vanilla wafers	185 g

1. Combine pudding mix and milk in bowl and mix well.

2. Slice bananas.

3. Reserve 5 cookies for garnish and spread half remaining vanilla wafers in 1 layer in 9-inch (23 cm) square or 7 x 11-inch (18 x 28 cm) dish. Spoon half vanilla pudding over wafers and layer half banana slices over pudding.

4. Spread another layer of vanilla wafers and remaining banana slices. Spoon on remaining vanilla pudding.

5. Crush reserved cookies and sprinkle over dessert. Refrigerate for 3 to 4 hours before serving.

Nutrition Facts
Serving Size ½ cup (125 ml)
Servings Per Recipe 8
Amount Per Serving
Calories 203
Total Fat 4g
Cholesterol 0mg
Sodium 439mg
Total Carbohydrate 36g
Dietary Fiber 1g
Sugars 10g
Protein 6g

Mandarin Orange Pudding

1 (1 ounce) package sugar-free instant
    vanilla pudding mix   30 g
1½ cups fat-free milk   375 ml
½ teaspoon orange or almond extract   2 ml
1 (11 ounce) can mandarin oranges, drained 315 g

1. Combine pudding mix and milk in bowl and stir well.

2. Stir in or orange or almond extract.

3. Carefully fold mandarin oranges into pudding. Spoon into 4 custard cups. Refrigerate.

Nutrition Facts
Serving Size ½ cup (125 ml)   Servings Per Recipe 4
Amount Per Serving
Calories 76
Total Fat less than 1g
Cholesterol 2mg
Sodium 336mg
Total Carbohydrate 16g
Dietary Fiber less than 1g
Sugars 10g
Protein 3g

Banana Dream Cream

1 (6 ounce) carton reduced-fat
    banana-flavored yogurt   170 g
1 large banana, peeled, sliced
1 cup fat-free whipped topping, thawed   75 g
Ground nutmeg or ground mace

1. Stir yogurt and banana in small bowl. Fold in whipped topping. Divide evenly in 4 dessert dishes and refrigerate for at least 30 minutes.

2. Sprinkle with ground nutmeg or mace before serving.

Nutrition Facts
Serving Size: ½ cup (125 ml)   Servings Per Recipe 4
Amount Per Serving
Calories 69
Total Fat 1g
Cholesterol 1mg
Sodium 59mg
Total Carbohydrate 13g
Dietary Fiber 1g
Sugars 9g
Protein 6g

Cherry-Almond Tapioca Pudding

4 (4 ounce) cartons refrigerated no sugar
    added tapioca pudding   4 (115 g)
1 cup reduced-sugar cherry pie filling   265 g
2 drops almond extract
Sugar substitute to equal 2 teaspoons
    (10 ml) sugar
2 tablespoons slivered almonds, toasted   20 g

1. Transfer tapioca from cartons to 4 serving dishes.

2. Combine pie filling, almond extract and sugar substitute in bowl. Spoon one-fourth on each serving and sprinkle each serving with one-fourth almonds.

Nutrition Facts	
Serving Size ¾ cup (175 ml)	
Servings Per Recipe 4	
Amount Per Serving	
Calories 141	
Total Fat 5g	
Cholesterol 15mg	
Sodium 30mg	
Total Carbohydrate 18g	
Dietary Fiber 5g	
Sugars 8g	
Protein 4g	

Spicy Pumpkin Pudding

1 cup canned solid-pack pumpkin	245 g
3 cups fat-free milk	750 ml
2 (.9 ounce) packages sugar-free cook-and-serve vanilla pudding mix	2 (25 g)
1 teaspoon pumpkin pie spice	5 ml

1. Measure pumpkin to have ready before cooking pudding.

2. Pour milk in heavy 2-quart (2 L) saucepan and stir in pudding mix and pumpkin pie spice. Cook over medium heat, stirring constantly until mixture comes to a full boil. Mixture will be thick.

3. Remove from heat and immediately stir in pumpkin.

Nutrition Facts	
Serving Size ½ cup (125 ml) Servings Per Recipe 8	
Amount Per Serving	
Calories 61	
Total Fat less than 1g	
Cholesterol 2mg	
Sodium 151mg	
Total Carbohydrate 12g	
Dietary Fiber less than 1g	
Sugars 10g	
Protein 3g	

Cream Cheese-Chocolate Cups

4 ounces reduced-fat cream cheese	115 g
1 (1 ounce) package sugar-free instant chocolate pudding mix	30 g
2 cups fat-free milk	500 ml
¼ cup chopped pecans, toasted	30 g

1. Beat cream cheese in bowl until very smooth.

2. In separate bowl, combine pudding mix and milk and mix well.

3. Add pudding to cream cheese and gently stir or swirl to mix. Fold in pecans.

4. Spoon mixture into 6 custard cups.

Nutrition Facts
Serving Size 1 custard cup
Servings Per Recipe 6
Amount Per Serving
Calories 97
Total Fat 6g
Cholesterol 12mg
Sodium 242mg
Total Carbohydrate 8g
Dietary Fiber less than 1g
Sugars 3g
Protein 4g

Coconut-Topped Banana Cream

Yum!

1 (.9 ounce) package sugar-free instant banana cream pudding mix	**25 g**
1½ cups fat-free milk	**375 ml**
1 (8 ounce) carton reduced-fat whipped topping, thawed	**230 g**
¼ cup (lightly packed) flaked coconut, toasted	**20 g**

1. Whisk pudding mix and milk in bowl until they thicken. Refrigerate for about 10 minutes.

2. Remove and fold in whipped topping. Spoon into glass bowl and sprinkle toasted coconut on top.

TIP: Toasted coconut is a real treat when you are watching carbohydrates. To toast, spread coconut in a single layer in a shallow baking pan. Bake at 350° (175° C) for 5 to 10 minutes or until light golden brown. Stir frequently and check to see that coconut does not burn.

Nutrition Facts
Serving Size ½ cup (125 ml)
Servings Per Recipe 8
Amount Per Serving
Calories 140
Total Fat 7g
Cholesterol 0mg
Sodium 155mg
Total Carbohydrate 16g
Dietary Fiber 0g
Sugars 6g
Protein 2g

Dreamy Pineapple Dessert

1 (1 ounce) package sugar free instant
    vanilla pudding mix   30 g
1 (15 ounce) can crushed pineapple with juice   425 g
1 (12 ounce) carton reduced-fat whipped
    topping, thawed, divided   340 g

1. Combine pudding mix and pineapple with juice in bowl.

2. Fold in one-third whipped topping at a time and lightly mix. Pour mixture into 8 dessert dishes. Refrigerate until pudding sets.

Nutrition Facts
Serving Size ½ cup (125 ml)
Servings Per Recipe 8

Amount Per Serving
Calories 51
Total Fat 1g
Cholesterol 0mg
Sodium 41mg
Total Carbohydrate 11g
Dietary Fiber 1g
Sugars 8g
Protein 0g

Creamy Fruit Dessert

1 (15 ounce) can chunky mixed fruit with juice 425 g
1 (8 ounce) package reduced-fat cream cheese 230 g
1 (12 ounce) carton reduced-fat whipped
    topping, thawed   340 g
Sugar substitute to equal ¼ cup
    (50 g) sugar

1. Drain fruit and set aside juice.

2. Beat cream cheese and 3 tablespoons (45 ml) juice in bowl. Fold in whipped topping, sugar substitute and fruit. Refrigerate.

Nutrition Facts
Serving Size ½ cup (125 ml)
Servings Per Recipe 8

Amount Per Serving
Calories 129
Total Fat 8g
Cholesterol 19mg
Sodium 107mg
Total Carbohydrate 13g
Dietary Fiber 2g
Sugars 8g
Protein 3g

Bananas Foster

3 ripe bananas, peeled
½ cup fresh orange juice   125 ml
2 tablespoons butter   30 g
⅓ cup brown sugar   75 g
2 tablespoons grated orange peel   10 g

1. Halve bananas lengthwise and brush with orange juice to prevent browning.

2. Melt butter in 10-inch (25 cm) skillet over low heat and stir in brown sugar.

3. Add bananas and remaining orange juice and cook over medium heat for about 3 minutes until almost tender.

4. Sprinkle with grated orange peel.

Nutrition Facts	
Serving Size ½ banana	
Servings Per Recipe 6	
Amount Per Serving	
Calories 135	
Total Fat 4g	
Cholesterol 10mg	
Sodium 1mg	
Total Carbohydrate 25g	
Dietary Fiber 2g	
Sugars 20g	
Protein 1g	

Key Lime Squares

2 (6 ounce) cartons reduced-fat
    key lime pie yogurt   2 (170 g)
1 (.35 ounce) package sugar-free lime
    gelatin mix   10 g
1 (8 ounce) carton reduced-fat whipped
    topping, thawed   230 g

1. Combine yogurt and gelatin in bowl and mix well.

2. Fold in whipped topping and pour into 9-inch (23 cm) square dish.

3. Freeze. Cut into squares.

Nutrition Facts

Serving Size 3-inch (8 cm) square
Servings Per Recipe 9

Amount Per Serving

Calories 88

Total Fat 3g

Cholesterol 0mg

Sodium 53mg

Total Carbohydrate 13g

   Dietary Fiber 0g

   Sugars 5g

Protein 2g

Grapes Fantastic

⅓ cup reduced-fat sour cream	80 g
¼ cup reduced-fat whipped cream cheese spread	40 g
Sugar substitute to equal 2 tablespoons (25 g) sugar	
½ teaspoon ground cinnamon	2 ml
3 cups seedless, green or red grapes, washed, drained	455 g
⅓ cup toasted slivered almonds	55 g

1. Combine sour cream, cream cheese spread, sugar substitute and cinnamon in bowl and mix well.

2. In separate bowl, fold cream cheese mixture into grapes until grapes are well coated. Refrigerate for 2 hours.

3. Spoon grapes into dessert bowls and sprinkle with toasted almonds.

Nutrition Facts
Serving Size ½ cup (125 ml)
Servings Per Recipe 6
Amount Per Serving
Calories 139
Total Fat 7g
Cholesterol 11mg
Sodium 29mg
Total Carbohydrate 18g
Dietary Fiber 2g
Sugars 14g
Protein 3g

Strawberry-Cantaloupe Bowl

2 cups (1 inch) cantaloupe cubes or balls   355
    g/2.5 cm
1 cup crushed fresh strawberries   200 g
Sugar substitute to equal 1 tablespoon
    (15 ml) sugar
1 cup lime-flavored reduced-fat yogurt   230 g

1. Evenly divide cantaloupe cubes into 4 dessert bowls. Sweeten strawberries with sugar substitute.

2. Spoon one-fourth yogurt over cantaloupe in each serving. Top each with one-fourth strawberries.

Nutrition Facts
Serving Size 1 cup (250 ml) Servings Per Recipe 4
Amount Per Serving
Calories 104
Total Fat 0g
Cholesterol 1mg
Sodium 49mg
Total Carbohydrates 18g
Dietary Fiber 1g
Sugars 17g
Protein 1g

Frozen Pineapple-Grape Kabobs

½ cup flaked sweetened coconut	45 g
1 (20 ounce) can pineapple chunks, juice set aside	570 g
1½ cups red or green grapes	225 g
16 (5 - 6 inch) wooden skewers	16 (13 - 15 cm)

1. Preheat oven to 350° (175° C).

2. To toast coconut, spread in single layer on baking pan. Bake for about 5 minutes, stirring frequently, until evenly brown. Watch carefully because coconut burns easily. Remove from pan and cool.

3. Place toasted coconut on dinner plate. Pour pineapple juice into pie pan. Thread pineapple chunks and grapes alternately on skewers. Roll in juice, then coconut.

4. Arrange kabobs on baking pan, cover with foil and freeze. To serve, remove from freezer and thaw for about 3 minutes. Serve immediately.

TIP: *For a quick pick-me-up snack, keep frozen grapes in freezer.*

Nutrition Facts
Serving Size 2 kabobs
Servings Per Recipe 8
Amount Per Serving
Calories 138
Total Fat 9g
Cholesterol 0mg
Sodium 6mg
Total Carbohydrate 17g
Dietary Fiber 3g
Sugars 11g
Protein 2g

Fat-Free Peach Sherbet

1¼ cups fat-free milk, divided	310 g
¼ teaspoon almond or vanilla extract	1 ml
Sugar substitute to equal ¼ cup (50 g) sugar	
1 cup chopped fresh peeled peaches	155 g

1. Pour 1 cup (250 ml) milk into ice cube trays and freeze until solid, about 3 hours.

2. When ready to serve, let frozen cubes soften at room temperature for about 15 minutes.

3. Combine remaining milk, extract and sugar substitute in bowl. Add with cubes to blender and pulse until chunky, then puree until smooth.

4. Add chopped peaches and pulse until mixture is smooth.

5. Spoon into 4 dessert dishes and serve immediately or refreeze.

TIP: Try with other fruits as available in season.

Nutrition Facts
Serving Size ½ cup (125 ml)
Servings Per Recipe 4
Amount Per Serving
Calories 43
Total Fat 0g
Cholesterol 2mg
Sodium 41mg
Total Carbohydrate 7g
Dietary Fiber 1g
Sugars 7g
Protein 3g

Delicious Devil's Food Cola Cake

1 (18 ounce) box devil's food chocolate cake mix   510 g
1 (12 ounce) can diet cola   355 ml
1½ cups fat-free whipped topping, thawed   115 g

1. Preheat oven to 350° (175° C) for 9 x 13-inch (23 x 33 cm) rectangular metal baking pan. If using glass, preheat oven to 325° (160° C).

2. Add cake mix to large bowl. Break up lumps with your fingers. Fold in cola gradually with large spatula just until it mixes well.

3. Pour batter into sprayed baking pan and smooth evenly with spatula.

4. Bake for 30 minutes or until toothpick inserted in center comes out clean. Cool on wire rack.

5. Spoon 1 tablespoon (15 ml) topping on each serving.

Nutrition Facts	
Serving Size 2 x 2-inch (5 x 5 cm) square	
Servings Per Recipe 24	
Amount Per Serving	
Calories 93	
Total Fat 2g	
Cholesterol 0mg	
Sodium 428mg	
Total Carbohydrate 18g	
Dietary Fiber 1g	
Sugars 10g	
Protein 1g	

Orange-Glazed Apricots

¼ cup reduced-fat butter spread   60 g
2 tablespoons orange juice   30 ml
2 tablespoons brown sugar   30 g
1 (15 ounce) can apricot halves (8 halves) in
    extra light syrup, drained   425 g

1. Preheat 10-inch (25 cm) skillet on medium heat. Add butter, orange juice and brown sugar and stir to blend.

2. Add apricot halves and turn to coat with orange glaze. Cook for 3 to 4 minutes or until apricots are hot and glaze well.

TIP: *For a crunchy treat, sprinkle 1 teaspoon (5 ml) toasted pecans or walnuts on each serving.*

Nutrition Facts
Serving Size 2 apricot halves (without nuts)
Servings Per Recipe 4
Amount Per Serving
Calories 129
Total Fat 5g
Cholesterol 5mg
Sodium 99mg
Total Carbohydrate 21g
Dietary Fiber 1g
Sugars 20 g
Protein 0g

Chocolate-Peppermint Yummy

1 (1 ounce) box sugar-free instant chocolate pudding mix	30 g
2 cups fat-free milk	500 ml
¾ cup reduced-fat whipped topping, thawed	55 g
¼ cup crushed sugar-free peppermint candy	45 g

1. Prepare pudding according to package directions. Refrigerate for at least 10 minutes.

2. Layer 2 tablespoons (35 g) pudding into 6 small glasses or custard cups. Add 1 tablespoon (15 ml) whipped topping and 1 teaspoon (5 ml) peppermint candy. Spoon in 2 more tablespoons (35 g) of pudding, 1 tablespoons (15 ml) whipped topping and 1 teaspoon (5 ml) peppermint candy.

3. Refrigerate for at least 30 minutes before serving.

Nutrition Facts	
Serving Size ½ cup (125 ml)	
Servings Per Recipe 6	
Amount Per Serving	
Calories 87	
Total Fat 1g	
Cholesterol 2mg	
Sodium 77mg	
Total Carbohydrate 18g	
Dietary Fiber 0g	
Sugars 14g	
Protein 3g	

Warm Pears Elegant

1 pear, cored, sliced	
2 teaspoons sugar	10 ml
½ teaspoon almond extract	2 ml
1 tablespoon toasted slivered almonds	15 ml

1. Preheat sprayed 8-inch (20 cm) skillet on medium heat. Add pear slices and cook, without stirring, until pear slices soften. Turn once and cook until pears are translucent. Sprinkle with sugar.

2. Combine almond extract and 1 teaspoon (5 ml) water and add to skillet. Gently stir to coat pear slices. Remove to serving plate. Sprinkle with almonds.

Nutrition Facts
Serving Size ½ pear with almonds
Servings Per Recipe 2
Amount Per Serving
Calories 90
Total Fat 0g
Cholesterol 0mg
Sodium 3mg
Total Carbohydrate 18g
Dietary Fiber 3g
Sugars 12g
Protein 1g

Fresh Fruit with Pina Colada Topping

2 medium apples (Gala, Golden Delicious, Fuji)	
2 tablespoons fresh lemon juice	30 ml
1 navel orange, peeled, sliced	
1 cup halved red seedless grapes	150 g
6 tablespoons pina colada-flavored reduced-fat yogurt	85 g

1. Core apples and slice thinly. Soak in 1 cup (250 ml) water with 2 tablespoons (30 ml) lemon juice to prevent browning.

2. Drain and arrange apple slices evenly into 6 dessert dishes. Top with orange slices and grapes.

3. Spoon 1 tablespoon (15 ml) yogurt on fruit.

TIP: *One teaspoon (5 ml) of toasted unsweetened coconut makes a great garnish for each serving.*

Nutrition Facts	
Serving Size ½ cup (125 ml)	
Servings Per Recipe 6	
Amount Per Serving	
Calories 60	
Total Fat 0g	
Cholesterol 1mg	
Sodium 12mg	
Total Carbohydrates 14g	
Dietary Fiber 2g	
Sugars 9g	
Protein 1g	

Strawberries and Balsamic Vinegar

Maybe you've heard about this unusual combination. Try it – the flavor is amazing!

1 pint fresh strawberries	360 g
1 tablespoon good quality balsamic vinegar, dark or white	15 ml
Sugar substitute to equal 1 tablespoon (15 ml) sugar	

1. Wash strawberries with hulls. Remove hulls and cut any large strawberries into halves. Add vinegar and sugar substitute and toss lightly in non-metallic bowl. Cover and refrigerate for at least 4 hours.

2. Remove from refrigerator and let stand for 10 minutes to remove chill.

TIP: *Wash fresh strawberries before removing hulls. If hulls are removed before washing, water will seep into the strawberry centers and may make them soggy.*

Nutrition Facts
Serving Size ½ cup (125 ml)
Servings Per Recipe 4
Amount Per Serving
Calories 25
Total Fat 0g
Cholesterol 0mg
Sodium 1mg
Total Carbohydrate 14g
Dietary Fiber 2g
Sugars 9g
Protein 1g

Mango Tango Tapioca

So simple and so delicious!

1¼ cups cubed mango refrigerated in extra light syrup, drained	205 g
1⅔ cups refrigerated no sugar added tapioca pudding	375 g

1. Spoon ¼ cup (40 g) mango cubes into each of 5 dessert dishes. Top with ⅓ cup (75 g) tapioca.

TIP: Add 1 tablespoon (15 ml) crushed, drained pineapple and top with 1 teaspoon unsweetened coconut on each serving for a special tropical treat.

Nutrition Facts

Serving Size ½ cup (125 ml)
Servings Per Recipe 5

Amount Per Serving
Calories 125
Total Fat 30g
Cholesterol 16mg
Sodium 138mg
Total Carbohydrates 21g
Dietary Fiber 5g
Sugars 14g
Protein 3g

Creamy Tropical Delight

1½ cups chopped ripe mango (about 2
    mangoes), divided   250 g
¼ cup fresh orange juice   60 ml
Sugar substitute to equal ⅓ cup (65 g) sugar
1 cup fat-free whipped topping, thawed   75 g

1. Combine 1¼ cups (210 g) mango, orange juice and sugar substitute in blender. Process until mixture is smooth.

2. Fold whipped topping into mango mixture. Garnish with ¼ cup (40 g) chopped mango.

TIP: *One teaspoon toasted unsweetened coconut or toasted sliced almonds on each serving makes a delicious garnish.*

Nutrition Facts	
Serving Size ⅔ cup (150 ml)	
Servings Per Recipe 4	
Amount Per Serving	
Calories 100	
Total Fat 2g	
Cholesterol 0mg	
Sodium 12mg	
Total Carbohydrates 22g	
Dietary Fiber 1g	
Sugars 16g	
Protein 0g	

Skillet Glazed Peaches

You'll think you are eating peach cobbler – without the crust!

2 tablespoons light butter spread with canola oil	30 g
2 tablespoons light brown sugar	30 g
2 tablespoons fresh orange juice	30 ml
1 teaspoon ground cinnamon	5 ml
1 (15 ounce) can sliced peaches with	
juice, drained	425 g

1. Preheat 8-inch (20 cm) skillet over medium heat. Melt spread and stir in brown sugar. When it bubbles, add orange juice and cinnamon.

2. Add peaches and cook for about 5 minutes until peaches are coated. When peaches are hot and glazed, remove from heat and spoon into 3 dessert dishes.

3. Serve warm.

Nutrition Facts
Serving Size ½ cup (125 ml)
Servings Per Recipe 3
Amount Per Serving
Calories 53
Total Fat 2g
Cholesterol 2mg
Sodium 34mg
Total Carbohydrate 9g
Dietary Fiber 0g
Sugars 8g
Protein 0g

Reduced-Sugar Diet Soda Cake

1 (18 ounce) box reduced-sugar yellow cake mix   510 g
1 (12 ounce) can diet lemon-lime soda   355 ml
1½ cups fat-free whipped topping, thawed,
    divided   115 g

1. Preheat oven to 350° (175° C) for 9 x 13-inch (23 x 33 cm) rectangular metal baking pan. If using glass, preheat oven to 325° (160° C).

2. Add cake mix to large bowl. Break up lumps with your fingers. Fold soda into cake mix gradually with large spatula just until it mixes well.

3. Pour batter into sprayed baking pan and smooth evenly with spatula.

4. Bake for 30 minutes or until toothpick inserted in center comes out clean. Cool on wire rack.

5. Garnish each piece with 1 tablespoon (15 ml) whipped topping.

TIP: Warm ½ cup (160 g) sugar-free red raspberry preserves and drizzle 1 teaspoon (5 ml) on top of whipped topping. Adds only 6 calories and 2 grams carbohydrates.

Nutrition Facts
Serving Size 2 x 2-inch (5 x 5 cm) square with topping
Servings Per Recipe 24
Amount Per Serving
Calories 88
Total Fat 2g
Cholesterol 0mg
Sodium 159mg
Total Carbohydrate 19g
Dietary Fiber 1g
Sugars 6g
Protein 1g

Sugar-Free Lemonade Icy Treats

The kids will love making and eating these treats!

Sugar substitute to equal ½ cup (100 g) sugar
¾ cup fresh lemon juice (3 - 4 lemons)   175 ml
5 (5 ounce) paper cups   5 (145 ml)
5 wooden ice cream sticks

1. Heat sugar substitute and ½ cup (125 ml) water to boiling over medium-high heat in 2-quart (2 L) saucepan. Reduce heat to simmer and, if needed, stir until sugar substitute dissolves. Remove from heat, pour into large bowl and let stand at room temperature for 10 minutes.

2. Stir in lemon juice and 1 cup (250 ml) ice water. Pour into 5 paper cups. Freeze for about 3 hours or until partially frozen. Insert stick into center of cup. Freeze until solid. Peel off paper cups.

Nutrition Facts	
Serving Size 1 treat	
Servings Per Recipe 5	
Amount Per Serving	
Calories 38	
Total Fat 0g	
Cholesterol 0mg	
Sodium 0mg	
Total Carbohydrate 3g	
Dietary Fiber 0g	
Sugars 1g	
Protein 0g	

Peachy Keen Dessert Sauce

Absolutely delicious over ice cream!

1 large fresh peach, peeled, pitted
1 tablespoon frozen unsweetened apple juice
    concentrate   15 ml
2 tablespoons reduced-fat buttery spread   30 g
1 teaspoon ground cinnamon   5 ml
Sugar substitute to equal 2 teaspoons (10 ml) sugar

1. Slice peach and arrange in microwave-safe pie pan. Add apple juice. Microwave on HIGH for 1 to 2 minutes.

2. Combine spread and cinnamon in microwave-safe bowl and melt in microwave for 15 to 30 seconds. Stir in sugar substitute. Spoon over peach slices.

3. Microwave on HIGH for 2 minutes. Stir and serve warm.

Nutrition Facts

Serving Size ¼ cup (60 ml)
Servings Per Recipe 4

Amount Per Serving

Calories 50

Total Fat 3g

Cholesterol 3mg

Sodium 51mg

Total Carbohydrates 6g

Dietary Fiber 1g

Sugars 5g

Protein 0g

Strawberry Dessert Sauce

Great with "healthy" ice cream!

1 teaspoon cornstarch   5 ml
Sugar substitute to equal ¼ cup (50 g) sugar
1 (16 ounce) package frozen unsweetened
    strawberries, thawed   455 g

1. Combine cornstarch and sugar substitute in saucepan. Add strawberries.

2. Cook and stir over medium heat until mixture boils. Cook and stir for about 2 minutes until mixture clears and thickens.

3. Cover and refrigerate for at least 1 hour. Serves 8.

Nutrition Facts
Serving Size ¼ cup (60 ml) Servings Per Recipe 8
Amount Per Serving
Calories 24
Total Fat 0g
Cholesterol 0mg
Sodium 2mg
Total Carbohydrate 6g
Dietary Fiber 1g
Sugars 4g
Protein less than 1g

Index

Cookbooks Published by
Cookbook Resources, LLC
Bringing Family and Friends to the Table

The Best 1001 Short, Easy Recipes

1001 Slow Cooker Recipes

1001 Short, Easy, Inexpensive Recipes

1001 Fast Easy Recipes

1001 Community Recipes

Easy Slow Cooker Cookbook

Busy Woman's Slow Cooker Recipes

Busy Woman's Quick & Easy Recipes

Easy Diabetic Recipes

365 Easy Soups and Stews

365 Easy Chicken Recipes

365 Easy One-Dish Recipes

365 Easy Soup Recipes

365 Easy Vegetarian Recipes

365 Easy Casserole Recipes

365 Easy Pasta Recipes

365 Easy Slow Cooker Recipes

Leaving Home Cookbook and Survival Guide

Essential 3-4-5 Ingredient Recipes

Ultimate 4 Ingredient Cookbook

Easy Cooking with 5 Ingredients

The Best of Cooking with 3 Ingredients

4-Ingredient Recipes for 30-Minute Meals

Cooking with Beer

The Pennsylvania Cookbook

The California Cookbook

Best-Loved New England Recipes

Best-Loved Canadian Recipes

Best-Loved Recipes from the Pacific Northwest

Easy Slow Cooker Recipes (with Photos)
Cool Smoothies (with Photos)
Easy Cupcakes (with Photos)
Easy Soup Recipes (with Photos)
Classic Tex-Mex and Texas Cooking
Best-Loved Southern Recipes
Classic Southwest Cooking
Miss Sadie's Southern Cooking
Classic Pennsylvania Dutch Cooking
Healthy Cooking with 4 Ingredients
Trophy Hunters' Wild Game Cookbook
Recipe Keeper
Simple Old-Fashioned Baking
Quick Fixes with Cake Mixes
Kitchen Keepsakes & More Kitchen Keepsakes
Cookbook 25 Years
Texas Longhorn Cookbook
Gifts for the Cookie Jar
All New Gifts for the Cookie Jar
The Big Bake Sale Cookbook
Easy One-Dish Meals
Easy Potluck Recipes
Easy Casseroles
Easy Desserts
Sunday Night Suppers
Easy Church Suppers
365 Easy Meals
Gourmet Cooking with 5 Ingredients
Muffins In A Jar
A Little Taste of Texas
A Little Taste of Texas II

cookbook resources LLC

www.cookbookresources.com
Your Ultimate Source for Easy Cookbooks

Here's to your lifelong health!